GPC

(GlyceroPhosphoCholine)

Mind-Body Power
for Active Living
and Healthy Aging

the
vital nutrient
for
survival

Parris M. Kidd, PhD

Total Health Management Series No. 2

A *totalhealth* Publication
Published by Total Health Communications, Inc.
165 N. 100 East, Suite 2
St.. George, Utah 84770
Tel: 435.673.1789
Fax: 435.634.9336
www.totalhealthmagazine

Printed in the United States of America

Total Health Management Series No. 2

First printing, April 2007

ISBN 978-0-9793979-0-5

10 9 8 7 6 5 4 3 2 1

First Edition

Foreword

Welcome to *GPC (GlyceroPhosphoCholine) Mind-Body Power for Active Living and Healthy Aging,* the second in a series of totalhealth management publications. Parris M. Kidd, Ph.D. is an international leader in applying scientific principles to advancing nutrition-oriented health care. Dr. Kidd defected from "ivory tower" academia to the movement for better health care in 1983. Since then he has helped blaze the trail towards a holistic model of health and for integrating vitamins and minerals, nutraceuticals, neuroceuticals and immunoceuticals into sophisticated products to achieve, maintain and help restore optimum health.

As *totalhealth* science advisor for the past 11 years, Dr. Kidd has been an invaluable asset in keeping *totalhealth* magazine on the cutting-edge of self-managed natural health. He is a rare amalgam— dedicated scientist, concerned environmentalist, passionate humanitarian, highly regarded by his peers and a well-respected industry consultant. He is an excellent writer, sounding board and friend.

In his article "GPC, Nutraceutical Breakthrough for Medical Performance," Sept/Oct 2001, Dr. Kidd introduced GPC to the *totalhealth* audience as follows: "In these harsh times we find our daily lives more demanding than ever before. We are more challenged to process large amounts of information, to be more productive on the job and to make important decisions that affect our lives for years to come. Our mental capacities are being sorely tested. We have to perform whether we want to or not.

"Now we have help. GPC (GlyceroPhosphoCholine, pronounced *gli-sero-fos-fo-ko-lean*) is a nutrient that safely and naturally sharpens alertness, concentration and other functions of mental acuity. After extensive clinical testing GPC has earned its place at the forefront of mental boosters. Complementing its proven and reliable effectiveness is GPC's excellent record of safety. GPC is so integral to human nutrition that breast milk conveys generous quantities of it to the newborn. GPC is naturally present in all the body's cells and tissues, which feature makes it an orthomolecule. Orthomolecules are substances orthodox to the body: they are integral to the body's normal metabolism. Human cells do produce GPC however the constant high requirement and sometimes excessive demand for this substance make supplementation useful.

"So who besides babies can benefit from GPC? The answer is: just about everyone."

As Dr. Kidd explains, when GPC is taken as part of a broader total health management program, a self-help strategy for optimal health: "You, the reader, have a chance for active living, healthy aging, and a long and happy life."

Having taken both GPC and its sister nutrient PS (PhosphatidylSerine) for the past eight years I can attest to both its value as a daily supplement as well as its therapeutic impact on stress management.

Finally, it is important to acknowledge Peter Rohde, President of Science and Ingredients, Inc., for his commitment to sponsoring the research, sourcing the raw materials, establishing manufacturing standards and developing consumer awareness of GPC as well as PS. Mr. Rohde along with Dr. Kidd are changing lives for the better in a world of environmental stress and toxic stress. They are true pioneers in nutrition-based medicine; the only hope we have to save our current health care system.

Lyle Hurd
Publisher/Editor
totalhealth magazine
Total Health Management Series

About the Author

Parris M. Kidd, PhD earned his B.Sc. degree in Zoology-Marine Biology with First Class Honors at the University of the West Indies in Kingston, Jamaica, and his PhD in Cell Biology-Zoology at the University of California at Berkeley. His PhD thesis explored cell membranes in the fertilization process. Dr. Kidd entered the dietary supplement field in 1983 with a textbook on antioxidants, and is now internationally recognized for his work on phospholipids. He has been educating the professional and lay public about the unique phospholipid glycerophosphocholine (GPC) since 1997.

Author Acknowledgements

I am grateful to Mr. Peter Rohde for the opportunity to intellectually collaborate with him since 1987, for his partnership in developing and popularizing phospholipid products, and for his generous financial sponsorship of my phospholipid work.

I thank Mr. Lyle Hurd for encouraging me to write for the public, for graciously granting me access to *totalhealth* magazine, and for supporting the Total Health Management Series. I am indebted to Katherine Owens for formatting this book and for her other contributions to making it a reality.

Any intellectual product is a group effort. I acknowledge a great debt to the many accomplished scientists who trained me. Dr. Neil Hirschenbein, Mr. Peter Rohde, Mr. Lyle Hurd, Dr. Richard Passwater, Mr. Robert Crayhon, and many other colleagues offered constructive critiques that have enriched this text. Any inaccuracies or misstatements that remain are solely my responsibility.

Contents

Foreword by Lyle Hurd, Publisher   iii

About the Author; Acknowledgements   v

Glossary of Technical Terms   ix

Introduction by Neil Hirschenbein, MD, PhD   xi

1. GPC, Vital Nutrient for Mind and Body   1
   GPC Has Many Clinically Proven Benefits
   A Safe and Effective Orthomolecular Supplement
   A Vital Lipid™ for Survival
   GPC Works Together with Total Health Management™

2. Sharpens the Young Healthy Brain   11
   First Double-Blind Trial: Improved Attention and Recall
   Second Double-Blind Trial: GPC Proves Superior
   How GPC Could Boost the Already Healthy Brain

3. Boosts Brain Vitality at Middle Age   17
   GPC Improves the Physiology of Brain Functions
   Supports Natural Growth Hormone Release
   Slows Aging of the Rat Brain
   GPC Supports Cell Mechanisms for Brain Vitality

4. Helps Elderly Resist Mental Decline   27
   The Daily Nightmare That is Dementia
   GPC is Well Researched Against Mental Decline
   GPC Supports Total Health Management
   Preventable Risk Factors for Dementia

5. GPC Improves Stroke Recovery   38
   Stroke, Runaway Brain Killer
   What Happens During a Stroke
   Physicians Assess GPC Benefits in 2,997 Stroke Patients
   Using GPC Toward Effective Stroke Management
   Preventable Risk Factors for Stroke

6. Real Benefits Against Brain Trauma   49
GPC Can Partially Reverse Surgical Brain Damage
Success With GPC Against Traumatic Brain Injury
Protects Brain Injury Recovery in Animal Experiments
GPC May Help the Human Brain Repair Itself

7. How GPC Links Mind and Body   59
Excellent Dietary Source of Essential Nutrient Choline
An Excellent Body Reserve for AcetylCholine
GPC is a Unique Osmotic Protectant
Convenient Membrane Building Block for All Cells
Possible GPC Deficiency States in Humans
Supports Sperm Production and the Fertilization Process
A World of Activity in One Nutrient

8. GPC and Total Health Management   75
The "Structure and Function" Claims for GPC
GPC is Safe and Well Tolerated
How to Take GPC for Best Results
Total Health Management Will Amplify GPC's Benefits
The Top Ten Practices of Total Health Management

9. GPC Has Something for Everyone   83
For Active Living, GPC "Slows the Ball Down"
A Survival Nutrient for Healthy Aging
Likely Value for Autistic Children
GPC, Mind-Body Nutrient From Youth to Old Age

Resources   89
Scientific References in the Text   91
Appendix: Trials with Injected GPC   97
Indications for GPC as Injectable
Pharmacokinetics in Healthy Subjects
Stroke Trials
Cognitive Decline Trials
Growth Hormone Potentiation
Brain Injury Trials
Closing Comments

The Future of Phospholipids as Dietary   111
Supplements by Peter Rohde, CEO, Science & Ingredients

Glossary of Technical Terms

GPC Abbreviation for GlyceroPhosphoCholine

GlyceroPhosphoCholine (GPC) Pronounced *gli-sero-fos-fo-ko-lean*. A phospholipid substance present in all human cells. Unique by being present in the water phase of the cells. Found in small amounts in common foods, and abundant in mother's milk.

Phospholipid A class of substances with unique molecular design. Used by all cells to make cell membrane, and for other life support functions.

Orthomolecule A molecule *orthodox* to the body. Naturally a part of human biochemistry and found in all the body's cells and tissues.

Vital lipids Fat-soluble substances vital for health. Phospholipids, essential fatty acids, cholesterol, and the fat-soluble vitamins, all are vital lipids.

Protein A biological catalyst, made up of amino acids and able to speed up a chemical reaction. The proteins in cell membranes work in concert with the membrane phospholipids for optimal function.

Membrane (cell membrane) A very thin but continuous sheet of biological molecules. Made up mainly of a double molecular layer of lipids in which are located a great variety of catalytic protein molecules.

Cell The basic unit of independent life.

Metabolism The array of thousands of chemical reactions, catalyzed by proteins to maintain the living state.

Bio-synthesis The body's own biochemical processes that make the substances for metabolism and to otherwise support life.

Homeostasis The collective processes that hold the body's physical and chemical conditions within the ranges required for life processes to operate.

Stress Any influence that threatens homeostasis.

Stressor Any agent or factor that causes stress. Emotional stress fits in this category.

Physiology The array of healthy processes that support homeostasis. Such processes occur in entire organs or throughout the whole body.

Pathology Abnormal physiology—breakdown of homeostasis—at the level of cells, tissues, organs, or the entire body.

Baseline Level of performance of the subject being tested, prior to any experimental manipulation.

Depression State of low mood, often resulting from emotional stress. If continued over time, can become *clinical* or *major* depression.

Anxiety State of excessive concern over life issues.

Total Health Management   A personal commitment to managing all the factors that positively or negatively impact one's health.

Memory   The ability to revisit an earlier experience.

Cognition   Collective term for the sophisticated brain functions such as attention, concentration, memory, learning, and comprehension.

Dementia   Catastrophic breakdown of cognition, beyond just memory loss.

Stroke   Catastrophic brain damage from circulatory injury or failure. A "brain attack".

Traumatic Brain Injury (TBI)   Brain damage from a source outside the brain, usually a blow to the head.

Autism (Autistic Spectrum Disorder)   Lack of speech and/or social skills and/or other brain development.

Hormone Chemical messenger that helps the body's cells, tissues and organs function as a harmonious whole.

Transmitter (Nerve transmitter)   A substance released by a nerve cell that influences the activity of another nerve cell, or a different cell type such as a muscle fiber.

AcetylCholine (ACh)   A nerve transmitter that is unique for its widespread distribution in the body.

Receptor   A structure located on or in the cell, that triggers a specific cell response to a transmitter or hormone.

Growth hormone (GH)   A hormone that helps manage growth. Close to being a master hormone. Made in the pituitary, the gland that comes closest to being the body's master gland.

MRI, SPECT, PET   Acronyms for *Magnetic Resonance Imaging, Single-Photon Emission Computed Tomography,* and *Positron Emission Tomography.* These techniques help map the brain, with virtually no bad side effects.

Trophic (Traditional term in biology)   Supportive of growth; restorative; regenerative.

Growth factor   A small protein that stimulates and otherwise supports cell and tissue growth and renewal.

Introduction

S everal years ago I first heard about GPC. Obviously, I heard about it at a lecture given by Dr. Parris Kidd. Since that time my wife Mary Anne RN, CCN and I have recommended GPC to a lot of patients. Mary Anne takes it herself. She says, "I take it daily, and recommend it to young clients when they have an exam to take such as the MCAT, LSAT, or other. GPC certainly helped me when I was studying for my CCN classes and my Boards with the IAACN for the CCN certification. I took my Boards in 2004, and I and my fellow candidates, several of whom were Doctors of Pharmacy, took GPC 15 minutes prior to taking our exam. We all believe the GPC enhanced our cognitive performance on the exam."

Mary Anne and I even gave a lecture where GPC was a prominent part of the talk. Sharp Health Care asked us to talk on Supplements at their Annual Women's Symposium. After generally discussing supplements, I wanted to focus on just one nutrient—GPC.

I had several reasons for selecting GPC. The first reason was that so many patients are concerned about their memory, especially as they get into their forties and fifties, and have experience with family and friends with Alzheimer's disease. The second reason is that GPC has been shown to be of benefit for every one with a memory problem—seniors with vascular or Alzheimer's dementia, middle aged patients with age associated memory impairment, and even normal teenagers. The third reason, especially at a conference sponsored by a traditional hospital establishment, was the desire to present solid scientific research evidence of benefit. At that time there were many double-blind, placebo controlled studies that demonstrated GPC's benefits. I also felt that if I could demonstrate the significant science behind GPC, a nutrient that very few would have been knowledgeable about, imagine the data that exists for more commonly known vitamins, minerals, amino acids, and other supplements.

At the La Jolla Institute of Comprehensive Medicine, I have seen powerful benefits for patients with mild and serious memory impairment, as well as for patients with strokes and other traumatic brain injuries. I've always believed that you always start therapies with the safest compounds. Therefore I always start with nutrients that naturally occur in human cells and respond to human biochemistry. If that doesn't work, I will move on to herbal therapies and finally to pharmaceuticals. These therapies are always combined with Comprehensive Life Style Therapies. GPC is a safe, effective orthomolecular compound and can easily be combined with Dr. Kidd's Total Health Management.

All of this information is now available in Dr. Kidd's *GPC: Mind-Body Power for Active Living and Healthy Aging*. With very readable language this book will be of benefit for both consumers as well as medical professionals. Dr Kidd gives detailed information of the studies showing benefit for memory, in normal youth to demented seniors, for strokes, and brain trauma. He includes the scientific reasons for why GPC works—increasing acetylcholine, increasing nerve growth factors, and improving cell membrane phospholipids. He includes new information about GPC's other benefits—in maintaining osmotic pressure, improving male fertility, and potential benefits in Duchene Muscular Dystrophy. Since I read his book, I'm contacting patients with muscular dystrophy and having them add GPC to their nutritional regimen.

For patients and medical professionals who are looking for safe, effective, scientifically proven nutrients I strongly urge you to read about GPC in Dr. Parris Kidd's *GPC: Mind-Body Power for Active Living and Healthy Aging*.

                        ~ Neil Hirschenbein MD, PhD, CCN, CNS
                                         Medical Director
          La Jolla Institute of Comprehensive Medicine
                               La Jolla, California

CHAPTER 1

GPC, Vital Nutrient for Mind and Body

- GPC is a lipid vital for survival, even abundant in mother's milk.
- GPC is naturally present in the body— an orthomolecule.
- GPC uniquely supports life processes that integrate mind with body.

GPC or GlyceroPhosphoCholine (pronounced *gli-sero-fos-fo-ko-lean*) is a nutrient substance that occurs naturally in the human body and in almost all living things. GPC has been the subject of a great deal of scientific research. The clinical studies with humans found that GPC is an excellent dietary supplement for the brain. GPC also is safe for people of all ages, including the very ill.

GPC is an *orthomolecule*—a *molecule orthodox* to the body, meaning that it is part of the body's natural biochemical functions. This special nutritional status helps explain why GPC is so highly effective and safe as a dietary supplement. GPC is also unique for its proven support of *mind-body integration*.

GPC is particularly effective for mental performance, including attention, concentration, and memory formation. GPC's contributions to mental performance are based in the mind. GPC helps the mind coordinate with the rest of the body, to integrate the whole human being into one working unit. This property of mind-body integration makes GPC a very important dietary supplement.

GPC supports human health in many important ways. The body's GPC is a key starting source for the essential nutrient choline and the chemical transmitter acetylcholine, and for other orthomolecules important to human *homeostasis* and survival.

But GPC is more than a metabolic backup for other key substances. The GPC molecule on its own provides a unique form of protection to all our cells. It is located in the cells' water phase (*cytoplasm*), where it normally reaches very high concentrations without causing harm. This pool of GPC is used to support a great many life functions, all at nominal energy cost.

The large body of scientific research on GPC suggests it has a ubique importance for the human brain, to a degree not matched by any other nutrient (or any drug). I have been working on this remarkable nutrient since 1997, and I continue to be fascinated by its capacities to salvage function in the damaged brain, to sharpen mental performance even in people who are healthy, to give new vitality to the aging brain.

GPC is not formally a vitamin, and the body can make it from other substances using its own built-in biochemical synthesis processes (called "bio-synthesis"). But bio-synthesis requires using precious life energy that would have to be diverted from other life processes. Obtaining GPC from the diet is an end-run around this problem.

Though GPC is not an essential nutrient it is an excellent dietary source of the essential nutrient choline. Since deficiency conditions are known for choline, this nutrient recently was declared a dietary essential. The Food and Drug Administration of the United States (FDA) allows dietary supplements and foods to make claims for their choline content. Such claims are based on a Daily Value (DV) for choline as an essential nutrient. GPC supplements often qualify as an excellent dietary source of choline. This topic is further explored in Chapter 7.

The content of GPC in common foods is quite low, and this helps explain why dietary GPC supplements can make such a great difference to health. The body definitely needs ample supplies of GPC and all the other nutrients it supplements. This book documents the impressive range of health benefits from GPC, and explains why GPC as a dietary supplement makes good sense for people of all ages.

GPC Has Many Clinically Proven Benefits
While word of mouth can be useful and physicians' experiences are important, the strongest test of a nutrient's importance to human health is the controlled clinical trial. GPC was tested in at least thirty (30) clinical trials that I have located in scientific journals. These trials were consistent in their test data and in their researchers' conclusions: GPC benefits young people, the elderly, and everyone in between. It seems GPC even may benefit children with cognitive and/or behavioral problems.

GPC has been clinically tested in trials that involved close to five thousand human subjects. Almost three thousand of them were stroke survivors, for most of whom GPC was uniquely beneficial and may have saved their lives. Most of the research was done in Italy, but reports also from Poland, Russia and the USA all concur that GPC can make a big difference to the recovery of people with severe brain damage. Besides proving effective in its clinical trials, GPC has an excellent safety record.

Most of the clinical trials with GPC were randomized and controlled, and some of them were double-blind: GPC was compared against a placebo or another nutrient, sometimes even against a drug.

Figure 1-1. The chemical structure of GPC, glycerophosphocholine. Note its zwitterionic nature (positive and negative charge on the same molecule).

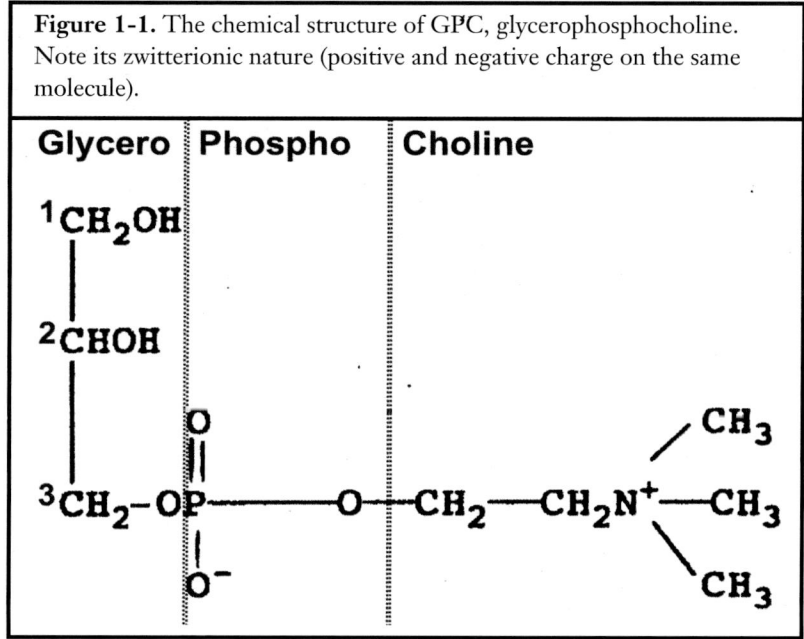

The double-blind clinical trial is the most scientifically sophisticated because neither the researchers nor the human subjects know who is getting the most active treatment and who is not. Though the double-blind trial has its limits, often it is the most objective way to evaluate whether the agent being tested truly has human benefits.

The many controlled trials completed with GPC document the following health benefits:
- GPC improved attention and word recall in young, healthy people.
- GPC helped cognition, mood and behavior in people with memory decline.
- GPC improved activities of daily living (ADL) and other quality of life measures in more than half the patients with severe loss of mental capacities.
- GPC improved recovery from stroke, as judged by several large teams of physicians in trials that involved almost 3,000 patients.

- GPC aided recovery from traumatic brain injury, including coma.
- GPC can be used to boost growth hormone (GH) levels in the blood.
- GPC can partially revitalize the aging human brain.

Impressive Conclusions from a GPC Meta-Analysis

An extensive body of clinical data has been published on GPC in peer-reviewed scientific journals. These data are sufficient for a "meta-analysis" of GPC's health benefits. Meta-analysis uses established statistical techniques to combine the data from multiple clinical trials into a single set of data that should carry more meaning than any one of the clinical trials. Professor Lucilla Parnetti published one such meta-analysis on GPC for dementia and stroke recovery. [1]

From her meta-analysis, Professor Parnetti concluded GPC was definitely useful against cognitive decline related to dementia. She also concluded GPC was clinically valuable for recovery from stroke. She stated, "...published clinical data collectively suggest a clinical efficacy of this cholinergic precursor in cognitive impairment..."[1]

The details of Prof. Parnetti's clinical meta-analysis will be covered in Chapters 4 and 5. GPC's established benefits for young, healthy people, covered in Chapter 2, add further intrigue to its potential as a dietary supplement. These clinical data are consistent with other lines of evidence—from human studies, from animal experiments, from biochemistry—that GPC is an exceptional nutrient for the aging brain. The science behind GPC suggests it is a nutrient useful both for active living and to support the healthy aging process.

What's in the Name GPC?

The scientific literature contains many different names for GPC. The most modern and correct name is glycerophosphocholine, or more technically glycero(3)phosphocholine, from which comes GPC. This name was set by the International Union of Pure and Applied Chemists (IUPAC), acting together with the International Union of Biochemists (IUB). These groups work by consensus to develop the authoritative IUPAC-IUB Nomenclature respected by scientists worldwide. Many other names have been used for GPC, including glycerylphosphorylcholine and L-alpha-glycerylphosphorylcholine. The term glyceryl- has now been replaced by glycerol-, according to IUPAC-IUB. The "L-alpha-" seen on some dietary supplement labels is outmoded. Also outmoded are the names choline alfoscerate and choline alphoscerate.

A Safe and Effective Orthomolecular Nutrient

GPC as a dietary supplement has the twin virtues of being highly beneficial to health and having no life-threatening side effects. Its highly favorable "benefit-risk profile" sets GPC apart from the typical pharmaceutical drug and from many of the widely promoted herbal extracts. This enviable record of safety and efficacy is closely related to GPC being an orthomolecule.

Orthomolecule is not a household word, though it should be. It does roll off the tongue better than lots of other words. It was brought into the English vocabulary back in 1968. That was when Professor Linus Pauling, the great biological chemist and two-time Nobel Prize winner, conceived of molecules orthodox to the body, or "right" for the body, out of which came orthomolecule.[2] By Pauling's clear definition, an orthomolecule is a substance that is naturally part of the body's healthy biochemistry.

In his landmark paper in the prestigious journal *Science*,[2] Professor Pauling made a convincing argument that orthomolecules should make exceptionally safe dietary supplements precisely because they are biochemically familiar to the body. He also reasoned that their biochemical intimacy with living cells gives orthomolecules greater importance for life than do substances that are not naturally a part of the body's biochemistry. These factors help account for the generally excellent benefit-risk profiles of orthomolecules.

Out of this brilliant realization Pauling founded a new field, orthomolecular medicine, for the purposes of:

> The achievement and preservation of the best health and the treatment of disease by varying the concentrations of substances that are normally present in the human body and are required for health.
> — Pauling L, 1968.[2]

The orthomolecular concept had an immediate impact on the practice of medicine. Compassionate physicians began to implement Pauling's orthomolecular principles and soon were reporting greater success with their patients. In the decades since then, vitamins and other orthomolecules have increasingly come into vogue for treating all kinds of diseases that previously were considered impossible to manage.

Orthomolecular medicine is now a thriving subfield of integrative medicine. A skilled physician can employ orthomolecules as dietary supplements to almost totally replace the need for toxic drugs. Often orthomolecular therapies heal the patient after drugs have failed to do so. Dr. Richard Kunin, an accomplished proponent of modern orthomolecular medicine, expressed its healing potential with great clarity:

> The orthomolecular strategy aims to diagnose and treat medical disorders in relation to mal-nutrition, pollution, and stress and to use nutrient balancing, detoxification, and hormonal supplementation as a means to restore the physiological mechanisms of healing. Even in the advanced stages of disease, where tissues and organs have been damaged, there is almost always an adaptational component that can improve with orthomolecular therapy!
>
> ⤙ Kunin R, MD.[3]

The body relies heavily on its complement of orthomolecules. After all, most of them were already integral to life processes in the simple life forms that existed billions of years ago. Given their fundamental contributions to life processes, most of these dating back to the dawn of life, it makes good sense that orthomolecules are more effective and make safer dietary supplements than molecules not integral to our life processes.

GPC is one of the orthomolecules that dates all the way back to the most primitive cells. Human breast milk contains an ample amount of GPC, which testifies to its fundamental importance to human life.[4] This and the other known roles of GPC in human biochemistry strongly suggest that GPC is a vital nutrient for survival.

A Vital Lipid™ for Survival

Chemically GPC is a phospholipid nutrient (pronounced *fos-fo-lip-id*). Phospholipids (PL, for short) are orthomolecules that serve a huge variety of functions in the human body. Some of their key functions are (1) as indispensable molecular building blocks for all our cells; (2) to enable healthy cholesterol management; (3) as emulsifiers to assist digestion; (4) as surface-active ("wetting") agents in the lungs, kidneys, and GI tract; and (5) as messenger substances.[5] The phospholipids are so essential to life that I decided to name them *vital lipids*™.[6]

The phospholipids are a subcategory of the lipid nutrient class. The term "lipid" is an operating definition for substances that mix into certain types of solvents. The lipid class is chemically broad, and includes cholesterol and many other steroids; triglycerides (commonly called fats), the omega-3, -6, and -9 fatty acids; and various other substances. Phospholipids are specifically lipids that contain phosphorus. Some "experts" call phospholipids fats (triglycerides), but fats they are not. The phospholipids are chemically very different from triglycerides, and much more biochemically versatile.

GPC is rather unique among phospholipids for being present totally in the water phase (the "cytoplasm" of cells). Since most of the body is water phase, GPC can get to very high levels in our cells and body fluids. All our cells have GPC, and having high GPC levels does no harm to them. To the contrary: GPC's presence is highly protective to our cells, tissues and organs.

GPC's great protective property is related to its rare molecular structure. Endowed with both a positive charge and a negative charge on the same molecule (called zwitterionic, see Fig. 1-1), GPC gives the cell protection against osmotic damage, simultaneous with protection against urea, a major metabolic waste product. This is a unique protective combination from one nutrient. The brain uses GPC as an osmotic protectant,[7] and it is also very important for the kidneys, which must handle a lot of urea under ever-changing osmotic conditions. This will be discussed further in Chapter 7.

GPC serves another vital function by being a ready source of choline. This is a vitamin-like, essential nutrient that feeds many metabolic pathways. But in its free, native form choline is difficult for the body to manage. The GPC molecule carries choline as part of its structure, and this can readily be removed by enzymes widely available in our cells. GPC is a major body reservoir of readily available choline.

GPC makes further contributions to survival by elevating brain acetylcholine (ACh). Acetylcholine is a key chemical messenger and nerve transmitter, crucial for mental clarity and for the brain to coordinate with the entire body. Its importance for ACh makes GPC truly a mind-body nutrient.

Going beyond choline and acetylcholine, GPC is a highly effective raw material for cell growth and expansion, and for making new cells. These processes all require new cell membrane mass. GPC in the cell water is readily converted into a lipid phase phospholipid, phosphatidylcholine (PC), which is a key building block for cell membranes. The conversion of GPC to PC is done by enzymes tacking fatty acids onto the GPC molecule, at very little energy cost.

These various roles for GPC altogether make it a nutrient fundamental to life. Working at this deep level, GPC facilitates the

7

harmonious functioning of all our organs. The clinical studies with GPC as a dietary supplement prove just how much it endows mind and body with the tools for survival. GPC is a survival nutrient *par excellence*.

GPC Works Together with Total Health Management™

Taking GPC is an excellent means to boost the healthy mind, and to help recover waning cognitive functions. GPC can be safely used as a dietary supplement over the long term, and it seems to have a restorative type of effect, whatever the age of the individual taking it. But to rebuild age-ravaged or otherwise damaged tissue is not easy, so that just taking GPC without making other positive changes may not be enough. GPC should be taken as part of a broader Total Health Management™ program (THM).

Total Health Management™ is a self-help strategy for optimal health. In these modern times with their harsh mental, physical, and chemical stresses on the human body, a THM lifestyle helps empower us to maintain our mental and physical power against the constant daily challenges to our health. Through practicing THM the individual makes a total commitment to lifelong health.

Take brain health, for instance. GPC when taken daily for at least a few months has impressive growth-promoting or trophic effects in the brain. However, it is unlikely to do its best job if nerve cells and circuits are being lost at a high rate. It just makes sense that GPC would work better if the rate of brain cell dropout could be slowed, through less smoking or drinking for example. This is where THM comes in—THM takes into account all the factors that can positively or negatively impact our health.[6]

Over the past decade, I have published on GPC and on many features of THM in the pages of *totalhealth* magazine.[8] As I wrote the book on PS (phosphatidylserine), I developed THM in more detail.[6] The practicalities of THM and its relevance to GPC are presented in Chapter 8.

Through ongoing commitment to the THM lifestyle, and ongoing use of GPC as a dietary supplement, you the reader have a chance for active living, healthy aging, and a long and happy life. This chapter and the chapters that follow are presented with the sincere intent to make GPC more understandable and accessible to the millions of people who can benefit from it.

Figure 1–2.

Above: A generalized animal cell, showing the membrane systems
    and organelles.
Below: How the outer cell membrane is organized.

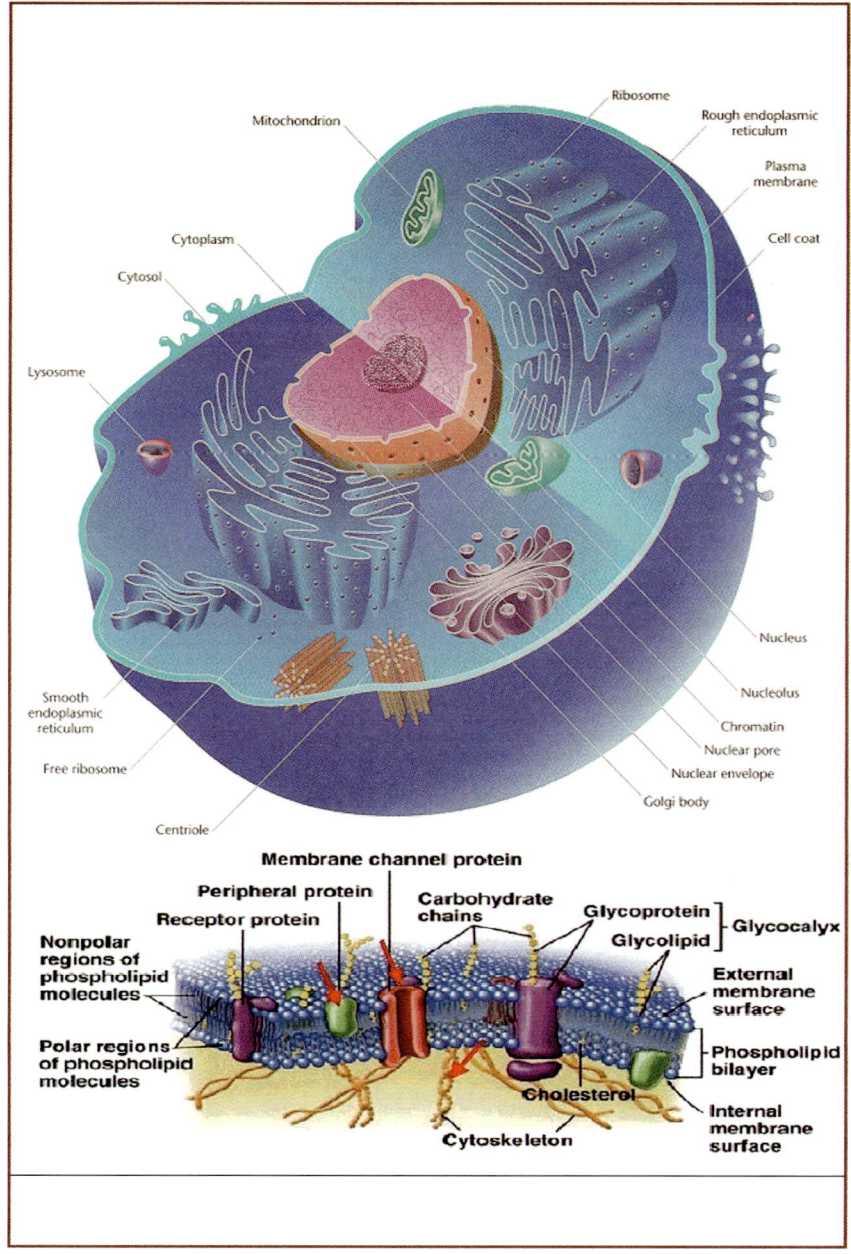

CHAPTER 2

Sharpens the Young Healthy Brain

- GPC boosted brain functions in young, healthy humans, in double-blind trials.
- GPC protected the subjects' attention and memory against chemical amnesia.
- GPC outperformed the drugs aniracetam and idebenone.

Who among us wouldn't like to have a sharper brain? Aging people are all too aware that they're losing sharpness, but young people also sometimes wish they had more brain power for challenging situations. GPC boosts mental performance in the already efficient, young and healthy brain.

Two well-designed double-blind trials tested GPC for attention and memory in young, healthy people.[9,10] Both followed a similar design and were done by Canal and collaborators at the University of Milan. Both trials were based on the well established "scopolamine amnesia" studies.

When administered by injection (or by mouth, scopolamine quickly brings on an amnesic state. This is a state of virtually total cognitive paralysis, one in which all the processes that normally detect and process information including memory, attention, learning, and other cognitive skills are impaired.[11] The drug works by blocking the action of acetylcholine.

The temporary cognitive impairment characteristic of scopolamine amnesia has similarities to the cognitive impairment that occurs in dementia. But it differs in two important ways: it develops rapidly (within 1 hour) following the scopolamine injection, and it wears off almost as rapidly (within about 6 hours) with no apparent bad long-term effects.

Knowing the exact dose of scopolamine that will trigger the amnesia, the researchers first gave these young volunteers GPC or a placebo over 7 to 10 days. Then they brought them into the laboratory, injected them with scopolamine and tracked them over the following six hours using cognitive function tests. Statistical analysis was then used to determine to what extent GPC could protect the mind against the chemical amnesia induced by scopolamine.

First Double-Blind Trial: Improved Attention and Recall

The first double-blind trial used 32 healthy men and women aged 19–38 years who had volunteered to be studied.[9] They were randomly allocated to 4 different groups. They were then provided with supplies of GPC by mouth (1200 mg per day), or placebo for 10 days. On the eleventh day they were injected intramuscularly (i.m.) with either scopolamine bromidrate or placebo. They were tested immediately before being injected (as a baseline measure) then again at 0.5 hrs, 1, 2, 3 and 6 hrs after injection.

In the mnemonic (Free Recall) test, 20 words are read aloud to the subject three times, then s/he has two minutes to write down as many of these words as they can remember. On this test GPC pretreatment significantly held off the amnesia all the way through the 6-hour trial.

In the test of attention (Cancellation Test), the subject is provided with a matrix of 60 rows x 20 columns of randomly generated digits; 3 digits are designated as targets and these must be located and eliminated within 3 minutes. On this test GPC held off the scopolamine effect for at least the first 3 hours. This meant GPC had a real but partial protective effect on attention.

The researchers concluded that GPC did give the young, healthy brain significant protection of its attention and memory capacity against scopolamine's temporarily crippling effects. And there was another, unexpected but pleasing finding from this double-blind trial. It was that GPC significantly improved the *baseline* word recall performance in these healthy young subjects.

The term baseline refers to the level of performance of the subject prior to any experimental manipulation. It's what we have before they experiment on us. The finding that GPC will boost the memory function measured as word recall suggests that the already good mental performance of young, healthy people can be racked up a notch, simply by taking GPC as a dietary supplement.

Second Double-Blind Trial: GPC Proves Superior

The second double-blind trial by Canal's veteran research group involved 48 men and women aged 22–33 years.[10] This trial resembled the previous one, except that this time GPC was compared not just against placebo but against the "smart drug" aniracetam and the synthetic antioxidant idebenone. Also, the subjects were pretreated with GPC pretreatment for a shorter time than previous: just 7 days prior to the scopolamine injection, rather than 10 days. In this trial the willing participants also take more tests, including: learning capacity for verbal and nonverbal material; selective attention; divided attention; and working memory. As in the first double-blind trial, the injection of scopolamine without prior pretreatment with GPC resulted in poor performance on all the tests—the predictable scopolamine amnesia.

Pretreating subjects with GPC prior to injecting them with scopolamine did significantly preserve (at least in part) certain of the learning and long-term verbal memory processes. Some of the cognitive processes partially protected by GPC were immediate and deferred word recall; facilitated recall; and recognition.

In this group of courageous people who volunteered to be temporarily disabled by scopolamine, GPC also protected "working memory". This was measured through a test of abstract reasoning carried out together with an interfering attentive task. The data showed that GPC almost completely protected working memory against attack by scopolamine.

In this second double-blind trial, the ample data confirmed that GPC's protection against scopolamine was statistically superior to aniracetam and idebenone.[10]

Experiments with scopolamine amnesia in laboratory rats mirror GPC's anti-scopolamine effects in humans. When rats were given GPC in their drinking water for 22 days prior to the injection of scopolamine, their memory and learning capacities were fully protected.[12] GPC also boosted young rats' performance on active avoidance conditioning, tests believed to measure learning and memory.[13] Therefore animal experiments reinforce the findings that GPC can boost mental performance in humans who are not old, brain injured or facing dementia, but young and healthy.

How GPC Could Boost the Already Healthy Brain

According to the findings from the two double-blind trials by Canal's group, GPC protects the young, healthy human brain against chemical amnesia. This is a rare accomplishment for any nutrient, and so far exceeds any pharmaceutical drug. Indeed, the two pharmaceutical agents included in the second trial performed inferior to GPC.

What Statistical p Values Mean

Science is humanity's best effort to systematize our subjective observations. Statistics helps bring these subjective observations closer to being objective.

No observation can be guaranteed 100% correct with a zero chance of being wrong. Statistical methods were developed to generate probabilities of being correct. Thus in any controlled scientific experiment, including human clinical trials, the data collected are statistically processed then transformed into the simpler p (probability) values.

Among life science researchers, usually the highest acceptable probability that an observation could be wrong is 5%. This calls for accepting a maximum $p<0.05$ ("p less than 0.05"), meaning less than 5% (5 chances in 100) that the observation is wrong and greater than 95% (95 chances in 100) that the observation is right. The $p<0.05$ value is often simply termed "statistically significant." A $p<0.01$ probability value would be nicer, since it means a 99% chance of being right and only a 1% chance of being wrong. This is usually termed "highly statistically significant." Then comes the $p<0.001$ value (99.9% versus 0.1%). Occasionally p values come out lower, and the lower they go the greater the chance that particular observation could be right.

Another impressive finding in these trials was that GPC improved the already efficient mental performance of the young healthy person. So, just how might GPC accomplish these powerful feats?
We do not know all that GPC is doing for the human body, but some of its clinical benefits clearly are related to building up the brain's stores of choline and acetylcholine.

Studies with rats established that GPC taken by mouth rapidly raises choline in the brain.[14] As choline rises in the brain, this likely can raise acetylcholine as well.[15] Acetylcholine is known to be fundamentally important for attention, memory formation, and pretty much the whole spectrum of information detection and processing. The finding that GPC can raise the baseline of youthful information processing suggests that some young, apparently healthy people are not producing an optimal amount of ACh in their brains.

Other animal experiments suggest other mechanisms. One is that GPC improves the sensitivities of the receptors on the surface membranes of the nerve cells, perhaps by boosting phospholipid renewal in the membrane. Another is that GPC may improve the fluidity of cell membranes, by combining with omega-3 fatty acids such as the DHA and EPA found in fish oil supplements. The biochemical actions of GPC will be explored in Chapter 7.

In summary, the evidence that GPC can improve already competent mental performance in young, healthy people elevates it to a special category of nutrient. This unique capacity for benefit adds further to GPC's track record over more than a decade of use, as a safe and well tolerated orthomolecular nutrient. GPC is a tried and true dietary supplement, able to benefit active living in the young. The next chapter reviews GPC's benefits for those not so young.

CHAPTER 3

Boosts Brain Vitality
at Middle Age

- GPC can improve key measures of mental performance in aging humans.
- GPC can boost natural growth hormone release in young and old humans.
- GPC as a dietary supplement slows brain aging in rats.

The focus now moves from using GPC to supercharge the healthy young brain, toward aiding the brain that is no longer young and is showing signs of wear and tear. Most of these people are over the age of 50, but some who have not lived a healthy lifestyle can notice their brain deteriorating after they reach the BIG 4-0, or even at an earlier age.

Some people who have taken pretty good care of themselves still develop brain problems as they get into their fifties. This reminds us that it's not always just about lifestyle. Just having to live in the modern world is stressful, generating not only emotional stress but chemical and physical stress as well. Considering how much stress we all experience, it is no wonder premature brain decline in people over 50 has reached near-epidemic proportions! Still, GPC and Total Health Management have a lot to offer in the ongoing struggle to stay mentally sharp.

Along with its sister phospholipid PS (phosphatidylserine)[6,] GPC has a proven track record against age related decline and other brain damage. These are the two most clinically proven brain nutrients, and both are widely needed, especially since there are no pharmaceuticals available that provide lasting benefit against cognitive decline. The sad realities, of dementia being epidemic and treatments for dementia still so limited, make it a moral imperative to explore all possibilities for relief.

In the intense focus on developing therapies against brain decline, for some reason nutrients have been neglected. Yet nutrients are available that really ought to be explored ahead of pharmaceuticals, since there is evidence they are helpful, they are far safer, and their benefits can be amplified by using them in combinations. For some of the worst challenges of modern life (dementia being one), nutrients work better than the available pharmaceuticals and often can safely be taken along with the prescribed pharmaceuticals. And of course, nutrients are almost always kinder to the wallet than are pharmaceuticals.

GPC has been tested in a number of controlled clinical trials for subjects aged 50 years or older with memory problems. In all the trials GPC displayed measurable benefit. GPC even outperformed several other brain nutrients and "smart drugs," in head to head controlled trials. A number of well designed experiments done with aging rats add further support to the benefits of GPC documented in the trials.

The many published trials with GPC against dementia are covered in Chapter 4. This chapter covers the research conducted with GPC on subjects with less severe deterioration of mental performance. Studies with volunteers at this early stage of cognitive decline are important, because GPC is not a panacea for dementia and there are no others. The prospects for benefits from GPC are greater, if it is implemented before dementia can develop. The earlier a nutrient intervention can be initiated, the better the chance for full restoration of function.

GPC Improves the Physiology of Brain Functions

From various tests of brain physiology, GPC is shown to improve brain functions at middle age. For the purposes of this chapter "physiology" can be defined as the array of processes that support homeostasis. Physiology is normal to health and when it becomes abnormal, gives way to pathology. Nutrients usually boost physiology (they're much better at this than are drugs), and can be used appropriately to avert abnormalities that could lead into pathology. GPC is one such nutrient.

An Anti-Aging EEG Effect on Subjects with Poor Memory

ElectroEncephaloGraphy (EEG) is a highly technical procedure that can sometimes contribute to understanding brain function. EEG uses a number of electrodes strategically positioned all over the scalp, to pick up voltage activity in the brain as frequency ranges. The four major ranges are beta (approximately 13–31 Hertz), which is the fastest, followed by alpha (7–13 Hertz), then theta (4–7 Hertz), and delta (0.5–4 Hertz) that is the slowest. With the help of computerized analysis, the relative amounts of each frequency can be calculated as a percentage of the total.

Changes in the relative percentages of the 4 frequency ranges sometimes can be linked to dysfunction or pathology. Also, as the brain ages there is a tendency for the faster beta and alpha waves to decline, and for the slower theta and delta waves to become more dominant. It's been suggested that agents that reverse these changes may have "antiaging" effects.

One double-blind trial employed EEG to assess GPC in subjects with AAMI (age-associated memory impairment). AAMI is a condition that is diagnosed in people aged 50 years or older and is associated with higher risk for dementia in later life. In this trial done by Moglia and others at the University of Pavia in Italy,[16] four AAMI subjects received a placebo and five received GPC (1200 mg per day), taken by mouth for 3 months. Sixteen electrodes were used and recordings were taken for 5 minutes with subjects awake and at rest.

At 3 months (the end of the trial), GPC had increased the beta (fastest) frequency significantly more than had the placebo. The data for the delta (slowest) frequency showed a trend towards a significant lowering by GPC, meaning the difference between GPC and placebo was apparent but did not reach full statistical significance. The failure of the delta data to reach significance may have come from having too few subjects in each group, an obvious shortcoming of this small double-blind trial.

Despite its small number of subjects, the outcome of the Moglia trial suggested GPC could offer physiological benefit to subjects with age-associated memory impairment. Subsequent to this trial, Sannita presented additional data to suggest GPC lowered the slow delta wave in AAMI subjects.[17]

EEG research experiments done with rats back up these tentative human findings. In old rats GPC significantly lowered the delta (slowest) waves, as found with the human AAMI subjects.[18] When young rats were given GPC by mouth, again the delta frequency (slowest) was lowered. As with the AAMI human subjects, also the beta frequencies (fastest) were significantly increased. Feeding these young rats PC produced no effect. The researchers concluded that although PC is a theoretical source of choline for the brain, it must not be physiologically effective for this purpose. GPC did work where PC failed.

Improves Human Reaction Time, Visual Processing

In three other controlled trials GPC improved a number of other physiologic mental performance measures. Two of the trials included *reaction time*, which is linked to acetylcholine nerve pathways[19,20]; and *visual cortex potential*, related to nerve pathways for visual processing that mainly use the transmitter dopamine.[21] The subjects in these trials ranged in age up to 65 years.

Reaction time is a measure of the time span required for the brain to perceive and respond to a specific stimulus. Usually it is measured in milliseconds (thousandths of a second). Abnormally long reaction time seems a reliable indicator of age-related cognitive dysfunction. Abbati and collaborators did a randomized controlled trial that measured GPC's effects on reaction time. In this trial they also directly compared GPC against the "smart drug" oxiracetam.[19]

In their trial Abbati's group studied 40 male outpatients of ages 55–65 years, diagnosed with "senile organic brain syndrome of medium severity" (rather like dementia). After going through a detailed "psychometric" evaluation process to establish their baseline mental performance levels, the subjects were randomly assigned into two groups. One group received 1 gram of the "smart drug" oxiracetam and the other group received 1 gram of GPC, each by intramuscular injection, once daily for 12 weeks. Clinically, over the long-term one gram (1000 milligrams) of GPC given by injection into the muscle is roughly equivalent with 1200 milligrams given by mouth. After they stopped receiving the test substances, the patients returned for follow up testing over another 2, 4, 8, and 12 weeks.

At the end of the 12 week dosing period, the data showed that both oxiracetam and GPC had improved the subjects' reaction times, mental performance, and overall clinical status. But at the last follow up assessment, 3 months after daily dosing ended, the GPC group showed a more lasting beneficial outcome than did the oxiracetam group.

This finding by Abbati's group[19]—that GPC's positive effects had continued to improve 3 months after the patients ceased taking it—is a clue that GPC has trophic effects. The word "trophic" goes far back in experimental science; it suggests growth-supportive, restorative, regenerative.

Visual evoked potential (VEP) is another physiologic response that is reliably linked to cognitive performance. For this trial Sicurella and colleagues recruited 5 subjects of ages 59–83 who presented clinically with "chronic cerebral vasculopathy"—damage to the brain circulation.[21] The subjects were fitted with scalp caps that carried 28 electrodes, which recorded their brain's cortical electrical potential changes in response to visual stimulation. They were documented as having abnormally low VEP. Then they were treated with GPC.

Abnormal Mental Decline Signals Risk of Dementia

Poor cognitive function after the age of 50 is associated with higher risk for dementia later in life. Abnormal mental performance scores (on memory, learning, other cognitive functions) can be compared against a database for the subject's gender and age, then classified either as normal (whatever that means) or as abnormal to some degree. Someone who knows their mental performance is below normal does have options for salvaging it before it can progress to dementia. The earlier they realize they have a problem, the better their chances for doing something about it.

Stedman's Pocket Medical Dictionary defines cognition as: "the quality of knowing, which includes perceiving, recognizing, conceiving, judging, sensing, reasoning, and imagining." Dementia is diagnosed when these capacities are grossly affected.

AAMI (age associated memory impairment), ARCD (age related cognitive decline), and MCI (mild cognitive impairment) all are "conditions" that fall short of disease status but signal increased risk for progression to dementia. Being classified into any of these conditions means having a higher risk for dementia than others of similar age and gender.

As with all other functional decline in the body, memory and other cognitive decline is usually progressive. As the extent of impairment becomes more severe, there is less healthy tissue to work with, and the chances of rebuilding brain circuits become ever more slim. GPC may partially reverse this process, especially when used in the context of Total Health Management (THM).

It is our mental capacities that most make us human. When we lose them we're losing our human essence. If Aunt Sarah or Uncle Jim is becoming noticeably forgetful, they should get tested.

This was an "acute" human experiment. Each subject was injected intramuscularly with 3 grams of GPC, then their VEP was tracked for 5 and a half hours. The result was that GPC increased the VEP in all 5 patients, by more than 60 percent on average. Its physiologic boost of VEP began at 2–3 hours and continued beyond the fourth hour. The patients did not experience any adverse effects from being injected with the rather high dose of GPC.

GPC can therefore be credited with a range of positive effects on human physiology. Its abilities to (1) lessen the delta slow waves of EEG, waves that seem to signal brain aging; (2) enhance reaction time, and (3) enhance visual evoked potential; all help explain its clinical benefits for middle aged people experiencing declining mental performance. GPC may even boost the brain's glucose consumption, a measure of its overall energy production.

In a review paper that gave only sketchy data, Sannita claimed that healthy volunteers who received GPC (1000 mg) intramuscularly for 10 days showed increased glucose consumption in the brain, as measured by PET scanning (Positron Emission Tomography).[17]

Supports Natural Growth Hormone Release

Hormones are chemical messengers that help the body's cells, tissues and organs function as a harmonious whole. Growth hormone or GH comes closest to being a "master hormone" for the human body. Growth hormone helps manage growth, as its name suggests. It is made in the gland that comes closest to being the body's master gland, namely the pituitary.

The pituitary produces many hormones, but fully half of all its cells are dedicated to GH production. Once released from the pituitary, GH circulates with the blood until it reaches the liver, which picks it up and converts it to growth factors that have secondary effects on the other organs. The liver, kidneys, muscles, bones, joints and skin all rely on growth factors coming from GH to regulate their growth and renewal. Yet in humans, GH production goes into a steep decline not long after we reach adulthood (see Fig. 3-1).

Many experts believe that an accelerated decline of GH at middle age signals unhealthy aging.[22] Abnormally low GH levels, as compared by age and gender, are thought to contribute to hallmarks of unhealthy aging such as sagging skin, atrophied muscles, a potbelly, poor libido, and a host of other problems.[23] An intervention that would safely enhance the pituitary's lagging GH secretion "from the inside out" could make a lot of difference to quality of life in the middle years. GPC appears to be one such safe and effective intervention.

Normally GH is released from the pituitary gland under the control of a "releasing factor" that comes into the pituitary from the brain. It is called growth hormone releasing hormone (GHRH). Ceda and collaborators did several sets of experiments with GPC for GH release.[24,25] All are discussed in the Appendix, which

22

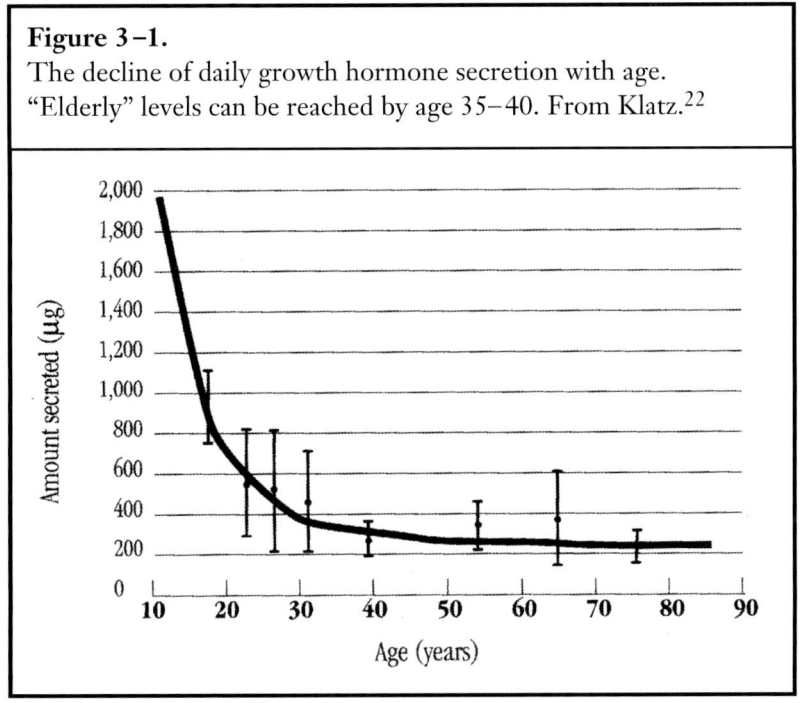

Figure 3–1.
The decline of daily growth hormone secretion with age. "Elderly" levels can be reached by age 35–40. From Klatz.[22]

reviews GPC as an injectable nutrient.

Ceda's group used healthy volunteers, young and old. They gave them GPC by intravenous injection before doing the usual triggering with GHRH (which also was given by i.v.). The pre-injection of GPC caused the healthy volunteers to release more GH in response to GHRH. When GPC was used, these healthy volunteers showed significantly higher blood levels of GH (see Fig. 3-2).

Ceda's group also found that injected GPC boosted GH release proportionately much more in the old volunteers than in the young volunteers. This makes sense because the baseline GPC release of GH is so much greater in the young volunteers—they naturally make much more GH than do the older volunteers. Still, the young subjects did show a substantial GH boost from being injected with GPC.

GPC may boost GH release when used by itself, without the usual stimulation by GHRH. In a small double-blind trial conducted by Schettini and other researchers,[26] GPC (1,000 mg per day) or a placebo were administered once daily by intramuscular (i.m.) injection, over a 3-month period. The researchers tracked blood levels of the stress hormones cortisol and ACTH, also of prolactin, and growth hormone (GH).

By the 3-month point, the patient group that received GPC showed significant lowering of cortisol and ACTH as compared to the placebo group, along with significant increase in blood GH. These findings ought to be confirmed with a greater number of subjects. If the need for expensive GHRH injection could be eliminated using a simple i.m. injection of GPC, this would greatly simplify medical protocols for GH therapy. It is quite possible that GPC could boost GH release when taken by mouth.

Growth hormone is often touted as a fountain of youth. Though it is far from that, many people could benefit from a modest GH "tune-up". Taking GPC as a dietary supplement over at least 3 months might be worth a try for this purpose. For practitioners whose patients are in deep trouble, working injectable GPC into the GH protocol would ensure the best benefits from GPC.

While investigating GH release by GPC injection, the Schettini team also scanned some of their healthy subjects using SPECT (single-photon emission computed tomography).[26] With SPECT they established that GPC injected i.v. did elevate energetic activity in the brain cortex, in 4 of the 9 patients they studied. For additional details, refer to the Appendix.

Slows Aging of the Rat Brain

GPC's seeming capacity to help revitalize the aging human brain is amply supported by extensive research on rats. A series of experiments with healthy rats, carefully monitored from middle age to old age, suggests GPC can slow aging processes in the rat brain. For rats and for humans, GPC may well be an "anti-aging" substance.

As rats pass through middle age their brains show structural deterioration. The numbers of nerve cells decline, the nerve circuits (bundled nerve cells) become smaller, and the numbers of synapses per unit brain volume also decline. Rat "intelligence" tests reveal functional cognitive decline occurring in parallel with the structural decline. A similar pattern of decline is seen in over-50 humans.

In a series of experiments done in Italy, GPC was provided as a dietary supplement to healthy rats via their drinking water. The experiments began at rat middle age, which for most rat strains is 18 months. GPC was given daily, beginning at 18 months and continuing over the next 6 months until the rats reached old age—24 months.[27] Rats were periodically sacrificed and their brains assessed in detail for structural changes.

The researchers did careful counts of the numbers of the different cell types in each brain, the sizes of certain key circuits, the densities of

24

Figure 3-2. Pre-injection of GPC (1000 mg, iv) boosted release of growth hormone in healthy older subjects. GPC used alone caused a modest release; GPC followed by growth hormone releasing hormone (GHRH) caused a much greater release than did either GPC alone or GHRH alone. The effect was similar but less intense in younger subjects. From Ceda, others.[12,24,25]

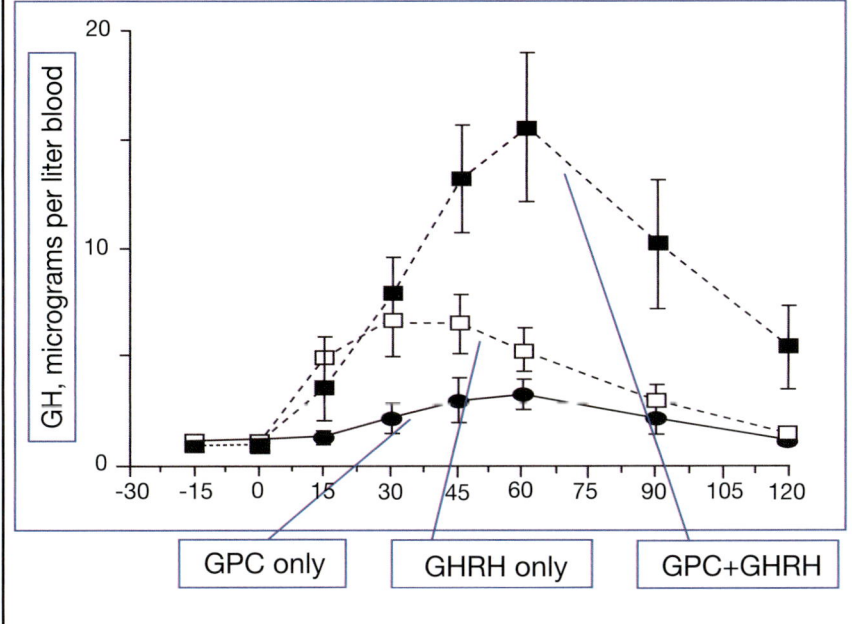

synapses, and other fine-structural features in the various brain zones.

This laborious quantitation established that GPC conserved the numbers of granule nerve cells in the cortex and cerebellum as the rats reached old age. GPC also conserved the Purkinje cells in the cortex, and the CA-1 and CA-3 hippocampus cells that are specifically linked to making new memories. In both the hippocampus and the cerebellum GPC actually *increased* cell numbers over the 6 months, while the controls lost significant numbers of cells.

The aging control rats lost nerve circuits in both the hippocampus and the cerebellum. But very different from the controls, the GPC rats showed statistically less circuit loss in both these brain zones. Giving GPC also protected against the synapse losses seen in the controls.

These rat experiments proved without doubt that at all 3 structural levels of the brain (circuits with multiple cells, individual nerve cells, synapses at the sub-cell level) GPC can give measurable protection against the losses that occur between middle age and old age.

25

GPC Supports Cell Mechanisms for Brain Vitality

In the rat experiments, GPC's protection of the aging brain extended even further than conservation of the nerve circuits, nerve cells, and synapses. GPC also conserved the nerve cell receptors for acetylcholine (ACh). This is a key to GPC's mind-body connection, because ACh is a universal chemical messenger that ties the brain together with all the other organs.

Supports Receptors for Several Key Chemical Transmitters

Receptors are little protein "antennae" that are embedded in the outer cell membrane and project out into the environment around the cell. Receptors for ACh are distributed all around the body, on the surfaces of many different cell types belonging to all the organs. Generally, the more receptors it carries the more sensitive a cell will be to ACh.

In the brain, the hippocampal cells have a high density of ACh receptors and ACh is essential for the hippocampus to make new memories. When GPC was given by mouth to aging rats, it partially protected against further age-related loss of the ACh receptors on the hippocampal cells.[28] Simultaneously, GPC had functional benefits by improving the rats' learning and memory performance.

By conserving the ACh receptors on these nerve cells, GPC partially blocked one functional consequence of rat aging. GPC also helps conserve the entire array of important ACh functions, in the brain and the rest of the body. Further relevant to its mind-body connection is GPC's partial protection of other nerve cell surface receptors—for dopamine, norepinephrine, and GABA (gamma-amino-butyric acid). All these major chemical transmitter systems are important for mind and body, each in their own special ways.

Supports Crucial Nerve Growth Factor Actions

Growth factors are small proteins normally produced in the tissues to coordinate growth, healing and renewal. Growth factors are one of the most exciting fields of research in the life sciences today. Growth factors for the brain are often called *neurotrophins*.

Nerve growth factor (NGF) works particularly to support nerve circuits that are cholinergic—that mainly communicate using acetylcholine. In experiments with aging rats, GPC as a dietary supplement supported NGF action by way of its receptors.[29] This topic will be expanded in Chapter 7.

All the mechanisms by which GPC works in aging animals are also operative in aging humans. It need not be surprising, then, that GPC's impressive "anti-aging" effects in animals are paralleled by its excellent clinical benefits for older humans, as will be covered in the next chapter.

CHAPTER 4

Helps Elderly Resist Mental Decline

- GPC is well researched against mental decline and dementia.
- GPC improves patients' quality of life and is well tolerated.
- GPC outperformed several other nutrients and drugs in controlled trials.
- GPC is a valuable addition to Total Health Management of dementia.

Decline of mental capacity is one feature of aging. Dementia is not. Normal, healthy aging features only a slight falloff of brain functions, as we see in the many centenarians who still have sharp minds. The severe memory loss that is now so common in industrialized societies goes way beyond healthy aging. Such dementia is disease—it involves catastrophic decline of brain circuits and losses of nerve cells on a scale very different from normal aging.

Severe memory loss, associated with other cognitive impairment, is known as dementia and is epidemic in the industrialized countries. The Alzheimer's Association of the United States estimates that more than 7.5 million citizens have dementia (see *Resources*).

The Daily Nightmare That is Dementia

The term *dementia* is related to "de-mens" (out of mind) or "de-mentation," translating as loss of mental capacity, loss of the capacity to reason. Imagine the devastating consequences of not being able to think for yourself or otherwise take care of your basic survival needs.

Dementia doesn't just happen. Dementia is the end result of years, probably decades, of progressive deterioration of the brain tissue (see Fig. 4-1). The disease of dementia marks a degree of cognitive deterioration so severe that social and occupational functioning is markedly impaired.

Along with the relentless deterioration of cognitive capacities can come deterioration of the personality. That previously mild-mannered, friendly, thoughtful relative can become aggressive, irascible, vulgar, the very opposite of what they were like as a younger person. The progression of dementia mercilessly destroys its victim's humanity.

As dementia progresses, the victim can become unable to recall the things that we all generally take for granted: what clothes they wore yesterday or the day before, where they went, what they ate, who they last talked with. They no longer recognize close relatives. As they come to realize that something is very wrong, they can withdraw from social life.

As the dementia progresses, the victim may reach a point where they have to be assisted with the most basic life functions, like eating, washing, going to the bathroom—known medically as the "Activities of Daily Living." The average Alzheimer's patient lives some 8–20 years after being diagnosed. Most dementia patients are taken care of by a relative until the end comes.

In addition to the tragic emotional costs of dementia, the financial costs to family and society are staggering. The Alzheimer's Association in the U.S. estimates that Alzheimer's care costs American families close to $19,000 a year, and that the total cost to the nation in healthcare and lost productivity could be more than $100 billion. Also, since more than 7 out of 10 Alzheimer's patients are cared for at home, the health and earning capacity of the caregiver also enters this equation.

All this makes abundantly clear that the best strategy against dementia is to prevent it from developing at all. But for those who already have dementia and for their loved ones, this option no longer exists. Their challenge is to slow the disease progression, hold onto as much as they can for as long as they can. They have to consider every possible means of meeting this challenge.

Despite the optimistic media reports from time to time, there are no prospects for a drug breakthrough anytime soon. The few drugs approved for dementia offer very limited benefits and often stop helping after just a few years. These drugs also carry the burden of serious side effects. By comparison, GPC is safe to take. It has been well researched against brain decline in the elderly, and has a track record of consistent benefit with no major bad effects.

The Alzheimer's Association estimates that for Americans aged 65 and over, the risk of developing Alzheimer's dementia is about 1 in 10. For those past age 85, the risk is as high as 1 in 2! Not good odds for any of us. The challenge is there. The strategy: diet, lifestyle, total health management. And clinically proven dietary supplements, including GPC.

GPC is Well Researched Against Mental Decline

GPC was used in 12 clinical trials conducted on a total 1,557 subjects with mild or moderate mental decline. In all 12 GPC proved effective. In 2001, veteran researcher Lucilla Parnetti published a meta-analysis of the clinical data then available on GPC.[1] This section discusses her findings, and Table 4-1 updates her list of trials.

Table 4-1 also shows that GPC was directly compared against the "smart drug" oxiracetam in 2 trials, and against the nutrients acetylcarnitine (in 1 trial) and citicoline or cytidine diphosphocholine (in 3 trials). In a total of 6 clinical trials, GPC outperformed all three of these agents.

Professor Parnetti's meta-analysis covered 11 of the clinical trials with GPC against dementia, that is, all those listed in Table 4-1 except the 2003 De Jesus Moreno Moreno trial.[30] The dementia could be vascular in origin, related to poor circulation (called vascular dementia, VD); or could be non-circulatory in origin (Alzheimer's dementia, AD), or of possible mixed origin with features of each. From her statistical analyses Parnetti judged GPC was clinically helpful for all three dementia categories: VD, AD and mixed VD+AD.

Very Helpful Against Vascular Dementia

GPC was used in 3 trials that were specifically designed against vascular dementia and involved a total 407 patients (refer to Table 4-1). To assess these trials Parnetti used mainly the Sandoz Clinical Assessment Geriatric (SCAG) Scale. The SCAG scale quantifies cognitive decline, emotional-affective (mood) aspects, and problems with interpersonal relationships.

Table 4-1. Clinical Trials with GPC Against Dementia. Updated from Parnetti and others[1] and de Jesus Moreno Moreno.[30]

First Author	Design	Patients	Dosing/period	Outcome
Moreno[30]*	Contr (DB) vs PLAC	261	Oral 6 mths	GPC superior
Vezzetti[20]	Contr (DB) vs PLAC	60	Oral 3 mths	GPC superior
Schettini[26]*	Contr (DB) vs PLAC	20	IM 3 mths	GPC superior
Paciaroni[31]	Contr vs oxirac	50	Oral 6 mths	GPC superior
Abbati[19]	Contr vs oxirac	40	IM 3 mths	GPC superior
Parnetti[32]*	Contr vs AC	126	Oral 6 mths	GPC superior
Frattola[33]	Contr vs citicoline	126	IM 3 mths	GPC superior
Di Perri[34]	Contr vs citicoline	120	IM 3 mths	GPC superior
Muratorio[35]	Contr vs citicoline	112	IM 3 mths	GPC superior
Ban[36]	Open	523	Oral 6 mths	GPC effective
Palleschi[37]	Open	99	Oral 6 mths	GPC effective
Bassi[38]	Open	20	Oral 3 mths	GPC effective

Total trials: 12   Total patients: 1557

* = Vascular dementia patients only. Trials not marked * had Alzheimer's dementia or mixed vascular-nonvascular dementias.

Contr = controlled; DB = double-blind; PLAC = placebo; Oral = by mouth; IM = intramuscular; AC = acetylcarnitine; GPC = glycerophosphocholine

By Parnetti's analysis, GPC statistically improved the SCAG scores and the overall clinical symptoms, to a "clinically important" degree. What she concluded:

❶ GPC significantly benefited attention, memory, and other cognitive functions.
❷ Fatigue and dizziness, other "somatic" (body) symptoms were improved.
❸ Mood was markedly improved including irritability and emotional swings.
❹ Also markedly improved were disorientation, and indifference to surroundings.

Measurable Improvements of Alzheimer's Symptoms

Against Alzheimer's GPC was used in 9 trials that included 1,150 patients (Table 4-1). Technically, this diagnosis is confirmed only through autopsy. Some of the patients had probable Alzheimer's dementia, others had a probable mix of vascular dementia and Alzheimer's dementia. From cognitive function assessments, typically these patients had mild to moderate dementia.

To assess these trials Professor Parnetti used mainly the MMSE (Mini Mental State Exam), which on a practical basis is hardly different from the SCAG. As with vascular dementia, for the probable Alzheimer's patients and patients with mixed dementias she concluded GPC had clinically important benefits:

❶ GPC significantly increased the MMSE cognition scores in all the trials. The MMSE improvement ranged from 10 to 26 percent.
❷ GPC improved attention and memory.
❸ Orientation and language markedly improved.
❹ Mood was improved.

Subsequent to the Parnetti meta-analysis, a large multicenter, double-blind trial was published from Mexico.[30] GPC as dietary supplement (1200 mg per day) was compared against placebo, in 261 probable Alzheimer's patients for 6 months. A number of internationally recognized measuring scales were used, including the MMSE, the GDS (Global Deterioration Scale, for cognitive decline), the ADAS (Alzheimer's Disease Assessment Scale-Total, Cognitive, Behavioral), the GIS (Global Improvement Scale), and the CGI (Clinical Global Impression). GPC proved significantly superior to placebo on all these clinical assessment scales.

The investigators who managed this well-designed, multicenter trial also found that GPC significantly improved behavior and ADL (activities of daily living), factors that are very important to the management of Alzheimer's patients. Among the 261 patients in this large trial there was not a single dropout due to bad side effects from GPC.[30]

GPC Supports Total Health Management

To conserve brain and mind and body and all the other features of good health, our best (and only practical) chance is total management of our health. As introduced in the previous chapter, and in the PS book in this series,[6] Total Health Management (THM) is a self-help strategy that is within the control of the patient who wants to do it. THM works best as a lifestyle of its own. THM should be a daily practice that is all the time taking into account all the factors that can positively or negatively impact health. Effective THM consciously integrates all the activities of daily life into a harmonious whole, urging body, mind and spirit towards health and happiness.

The people who care for people with dementia (or any other chronic illness, for that matter) also should practice THM. This will give them the physical strength and mental attitude they need, to do what they have to do without becoming stressed out and sick. THM conserves our biochemical balance, our cell communities, harmonious integration of mind and body. Relying on all this, the spirit can soar. Using GPC along with other safe and proven nutrients as part of THM will contribute to active living and healthy aging, quite possibly even to longer lifespan.

For the declining human mind, the still conscious brain, recent scientific advances suggest that it's never too late to intervene with THM. Current brain research is at a fascinating point: it's clear that the brain is far more adaptable than previously thought. In late 2005 I reviewed this paradigm shift in a professional article,[39] and in 2006 in *totalhealth* magazine I wrote a more readable article titled *"The Human Brain Can Repair Itself."*[40]

The human brain has a reserve cell stock able to specialize into new nerve cells—by a process called neurogenesis. These

Total Health Management (THM)
For a Long and Happy Life [6]

THM means living actively by:

▲ avoiding stress, and exercising body, mind, and spirit.

▲ avoiding chemical and physical toxic stressors.

▲ using nutrients to optimize the life functions.

▲ working with an integrative health practitioner trained to assess total health.

▲ making the lifestyle changes to support these activities.

▲ reserving pharmaceuticals and other potentially life-threatening interventions purely as a last resort.

In this toxic modern world, daily practice of THM is our best chance to experience our birthright of excellent health. Practicing THM gives us—whatever our age or stage of life—a practical possibility to cure, slow, or reverse biological dysfunctions that are obstacles to our happiness.

cells are the stem cells so often featured in the health news. The stem cells are pressed into action by growth factors, and GPC and PS are among the few nutrients known to support growth factor actions in the brain.

It's now been demonstrated in Alzheimer's patients that the brain retains the capacity to make new nerve circuits.[39] This important human study is described in detail in Chapter 7. But for neurogenesis to work at its best, damage processes ongoing in the brain should be curbed. And ample supplies of nutrients should be available, to support the newly forming cells and circuits. All this becomes more possible once THM is put into practice.

Preventable Risk Factors for Dementia
The first task of THM is risk factor recognition and prevention. Risk factors are factors that increase your risk for having something bad to happen to you. By practicing THM and taking GPC, the individual with commitment and attitude can lessen or get rid of

their personal risk factors, and have a real shot at regaining some of what they have lost.

Most medically recognized risk factors are linked to dietary or lifestyle habits rather than to "bad genes". Hereditary risk factors are far less frequent and important than are "environmental" risk factors that are subject to modification. This means that anyone can eliminate, or at least reduce, at least some of their risk factors for disease once these have been identified.

As the reader contemplates becoming more disciplined about total health management, it is important to understand that even the most heavily genetically loaded diseases can be ameliorated, delayed, or successfully managed by careful attention to modifiable risk factors. Simply to assume a disease comes from bad genes and therefore can't be treated, is an unnecessary and harmful mistake.

Let's look at a conservative assessment of risk factors for dementia, that is, staying with those factors most proven by science. This makes for a likely understated estimate. But even on an understated basis the dementia risk factors are considerable. So many are known that it's best to think of a dementia risk factor matrix (see box).

Dementia Risk Factor Matrix [6, 41]

Very Likely Risk Factors: Prior brain injury; homozygosity (two doses) of apolipoprotein E-4; advanced age; family history of dementia or Parkinson's disease; Down's Syndrome; alcohol abuse; depression, stroke, reduced blood flow to the brain.

Likely Risk Factors: Long-term coronary heart disease, emotional stress, smoking; pollutant solvents, herbicides, pesticides; certain pharmaceuticals; nutrient deficiencies, metabolic deficits; hypertension; underactivity (mental or physical); low educational level.

Think of the risk factor matrix as a multi-dimensional mix of the various risk factors. Each factor will vary in its time of onset, duration, severity, and relative degrees of interaction with the others. Each individual will have a unique risk factor matrix, because each of us is a unique human being. Each person's gene makeup will have unique interactions with their overall risk factor matrix, with the genes themselves being part of the risk factor matrix.

Brain Injury. This is probably the single most proven risk factor for dementia. The *dementia pugilistica* of brain-damaged boxers is virtually identical to vascular dementia or Alzheimer's. But it's really scary to realize that just one concussion injury to the brain can increase the risk for dementia in later life, to as much as 4 times the normal background risk. The more concussions or other brain injuries that occur, the greater the risk for dementia later in life.[41]

Apolipoprotein E4 (ApoE4). These are genes that in double dose substantially increase dementia risk. Homozygosity for ApoE4 (having this gene on both chromosomes) greatly increases Alzheimer's disease risk.[42] Yet ApoE4's "penetrance" (degree of control over the outcome) is far from complete. This means that many of the people homozygous for ApoE4 have a normal lifespan and don't develop Alzheimer's.

The two risk factors just described—head injury and homozygous ApoE4—can operate in synergy, to multiply the risk for dementia. It is well established that a person who sustains a head trauma has about a 4x risk of getting dementia later in life. Another person homozygous for ApoE4 also has about a 4x risk. But that unfortunate person who sustains brain trauma AND is homozygous for ApoE4 has about a ten-fold risk of getting Alzheimer's.[41] As to how much the other dementia risk factors act in synergy—we simply don't know.

Down's Syndrome (DS). This inherited condition is another highly probable risk factor for dementia. Yet many DS people are quite intelligent, and many never get dementia. Bad genes are no guarantee people will get dementia.

Hypertension, Stroke, Diabetes. All these are recognized as risk factors, supposedly more for vascular dementia (VD) than for Alzheimer's dementia (AD). Actually, experts find very little clinical difference between these two dementias. These 3 risk factors tend to occur together, tend to magnify each other (synergy again). And all are potential killers. Yet all are treatable and manageable through lifestyle.

Nutrient Deficiencies. Dietary lack of certain nutrients can mimic dementia. Most obvious are deficiencies of vitamin B12 or folate. Among people older than 40, there is a high incidence of stomach intestinal problems that limit vitamin absorption. Anyone with problems of this type should consider taking digestive enzymes.

Pharmaceuticals. Many prescription or over the counter drugs have toxic effects that can mimic dementia. As much as 10 percent of all apparent dementia cases may be induced by sleep aids, sedatives, antidepressants, or drugs from other categories.[43] Most are reversible to some extent, but only if the responsible physician is sufficiently alert to make the connection. One really useful reference book for this purpose is *Worst Pills, Best Pills,* collectively authored by the Public Citizen Health Research Group of Washington, DC, USA.[43] It is written for all to understand, and pulls no punches about the often hidden side effects of many legal toxins.

Emotional Stress. This risk factor for dementia has been grossly underrated. A clinical study done at McGill University in Canada tracked two groups of people for five years.[44] There were the good stress copers and the bad stress copers. After 5 years, the bad stress copers had statistically greater damage to the hippocampus. It is known from numerous studies with humans and animals, that the high cortisol associated with mental stress can kill nerve cells in the hippocampus and effectively disable this major memory region of the brain.[44,45]

Environmental Pollutants. Though the level of scientific proof is not always conclusive, many of the environmental pollutants are virtually certain dementia risk factors. Brain tissue is especially vulnerable to toxins of any kind, including cigarette smoke and alcohol, because of its high metabolic rate and very high content of polyunsaturated fats. The current massive contamination of the planet by mercury and other heavy metals, solvents, and pesticides and herbicides just about guarantees that industrial activity is contributing to the ever-increasing risk for dementia.[46]

The net outcome of dementia risk factors is to deplete circuits from the brain (for a graphic illustration see Fig. 4-1). At its peak performance state, which usually is reached in the early twenties, the human brain can have upwards of 10,000 connections for each of its approximately 100 billion nerve cells. This yields a "ball-park" figure of as many as 1,000 trillion cell to cell connections—perhaps a quadrillion separate pathways, according to the U.S. Smithsonian Institution. But as it progresses toward dementia the brain is suffering awesome circuit losses.

Consider the brain's cortex, for example. Elderly people in their eighties who are not demented may have lost up to

Figure 4-1. SPECT scanning shows empty spaces in the brain matrix where function is below normal. Left, healthy brain, imaged from the top, front of brain facing down. Right, Alzheimer Disease brain, in same orientation. Note the large network of empty zones where metabolism is abnormally poor. From Amen.[47]

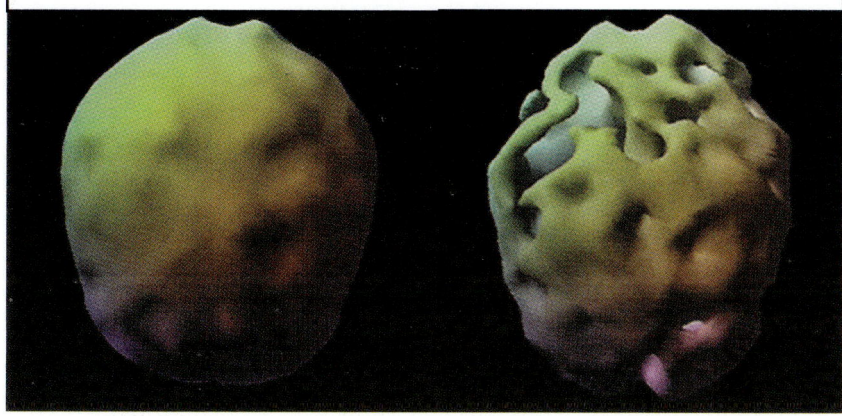

20 percent of their connections. In contrast, Alzheimer's patients upon autopsy can have lost up to 90 percent.[48] In the hippocampus, an Alzheimer's patient may lose just about all of the CA-1 cells crucial to memory formation.

No one can expect to escape this tragic fate unless first, they have eliminated their known risk factors for dementia, or come close to doing that. Secondly, they have to practice total health management with commitment and discipline. An important part of THM for the brain is nutrients that naturally occur in the brain, have proven brain benefits, and are safe to take. Nutrients such as GPC.

CHAPTER 5

GPC Improves Stroke Recovery

- Stroke or "brain attack" is a lethal event with limited treatment options.
- GPC has been tested in almost 3,000 stroke patients.
- GPC gave consistent and noticeable benefit for stroke recovery.

S troke, also called "brain attack", is a lethal blow to the brain, sometimes a mortal blow against life itself. At the present treatment for stroke is very limited: one in four stroke victims dies within the year following their stroke[49] (for more frightening statistics, see *Resources*). Those who survive longer are usually burdened with permanent brain damage. Several clinical studies done with almost three thousand stroke patients indicate that GPC makes a real contribution to stroke recovery.

Stroke, Runaway Brain Killer

Stroke is the third leading cause of death in the U.S., after heart disease and cancer—each year about 700,000 Americans are hit by a stroke. Stroke also kills a high proportion of those it strikes: In the year 2003 more than 273,000 American deaths had stroke as an underlying or contributing cause.[49]

Stroke also is financially draining, being a leading cause of long-term disability. The estimated cost of stroke to the U.S. economy for 2006 was $57.9 billion.[49] However huge the financial costs, these cannot compare with the costs in pain and suffering not just to the stroke patient but to their spouses, children and other loved ones.

In 1999, the latest year for which reliable disability figures are available, more than 1,100,000 American adults reported difficulty coping with functional limitations due to stroke.[49] More than a quarter of stroke patients are in a nursing home or similar full-time care institution. Most of the rest never fully recover and are cared for at home by loving caregivers. For most people with stroke the options have been limited: disablement and death.

What Happens During a Stroke

Stroke occurs either when circulation to the brain is restricted (the majority of cases), or a blood vessel in the brain leaks or breaks, hemorrhaging blood directly into the tissue.[49] In either instance the vulnerable brain tissue is catastrophically deprived of oxygen and blood sugar, and loses function within mere minutes.

The events of stroke are not very different from a heart attack, hence the term "brain attack." The result of deprivation of blood to the brain is a central zone of dead tissue at the initial site of the damage, surrounded by a zone of dying or almost dead tissue. Sometimes a huge segment of the brain can be functionally eliminated. In Fig. 5-1 (facing page), the apparent holes in the brain are zones where no function can be detected using sophisticated imaging techniques. This stroked brain imaged by SPECT appears (and is) hardly better off than the dementia brain portrayed in Fig. 4-1 on page 37.

How to Recognize a Stroke[49]

Warning Signs of Stroke

1. Sudden numbness or weakness of the face, arm or leg.
2. Sudden confusion, trouble speaking or understanding communication.
3. Sudden trouble walking, dizziness or loss of balance or coordination.
4. Sudden trouble seeing in one or both eyes.
5. Sudden severe headache with no known cause.

For the bystander, the American Stroke association advised at its February 2005 meeting to ask the possible stroke victim three simple questions:
1. Ask the individual to **SMILE.**
2. Ask him or her to **RAISE BOTH ARMS.**
3. Ask the person to **SPEAK A SIMPLE SENTENCE** (Coherently) (for example, "It is sunny out today").

If the possible stroke victim has trouble with any of these tasks, the bystander should seek help immediately. If the victim can get to a hospital within 3 hours, his or her chances of survival are much better.

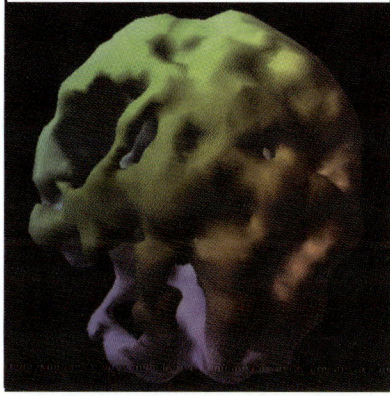

Figure 5-1. SPECT imaging of a right-sided stroke. Viewed from the top, front of the brain facing down. Note the extensive "holes" on the brain's right side (left side of the illustration). From Amen.[49]

Transient ischemic attacks (TIAs) are "warning strokes" that (supposedly) produce stroke-like symptoms but no lasting damage. The TIA often heralds a stroke soon to come, so that recognizing and treating a TIA can reduce the risk of a major stroke. According to the American Heart Association, 1 in 20 people who have a TIA will have a stroke within 2 more days and 1 in 10 within 3 months.[49] This makes it all the more important to recognize the warning signs of a TIA or stroke.

GPC has been intensively tested on stroke patients. From five separate trials conducted on almost three thousand patients, the more than 100 physicians that managed these trials were convinced GPC made a real difference to the speed and extent of their patients' recovery.

Physicians Assess GPC Benefits in Almost 3,000 Stroke Patients

The 5 trials that used GPC for stroke recovery all were published in scientific journals. They were not double-blinded—it was not ethical to give placebos to such acutely ill patients in a control group. Almost 3,000 patients received GPC in these trials (see Table 5-1).

All the GPC stroke trials used the same protocol: patients were started within 10 days after sustaining their "brain attack." GPC was given i.m. at 1,000 mg/day for the first month, then orally at 1,200 mg/day for 5 months. GPC produced very good clinical results in all the 5 trials.

Parnetti's 2001 meta-analysis[1] covered 3 of these 5 GPC trials against stroke.[53,54,56] All three research teams used the widely accepted Mathew's scale to assess functional recovery in the "acute post-stroke phase" (roughly the first month following the stroke). This scale assessed "cognitive domains" (awareness level, orientation) and "neurological domains" (language, cranial nerve function, motor and sensory function). In addition, 2 of these 3 trials[53,54] used the Global Deterioration Scale (GDS) to assess severity of cognitive decline and the Crichton Geriatric Rating Scale (CGRS) to assess behavioral functions.

In these 3 stroke trials, altogether 2,484 patients were treated with GPC. The single largest was the one published in the prestigious Annals of the New York Academy of Sciences. Led by Professor Barbagallo Sangiorgi, it was conducted at 176 centers of internal medicine, geriatrics and neurology spread all over Italy, and included 2,044 patients.[53] The Mathews, GDS and CGRS tests were used to assess the patients' progress in the "acute" first phase (month 1), then during the "chronic" second phase (usually 5 more months).

At 6 months, the end of their huge trial, the investigators judged that GPC had significantly helped more than 95 percent of their patients. They had carefully monitored their patients and found no life-threatening adverse effects from GPC. Nor did blood tests reveal any abnormal effects. About 14 patients were taken out of the trial (0.68%), mostly due to heartburn, excitation/insomnia, nausea/vomiting, or diarrhea. Headache was reported in 4 patients.

Table 5-1. Clinical Trials with GPC Against Stroke and Other Brain Damage.[1,50–56]

First Author	Design	Patients	Dosing/ period	Out- come
Auteri[50] (post-heart bypass)	Contr (DB) vs PLAC	20	IV/1 mth IM/5 mths	GPC superior
Barbagallo Sangiorgi[53] (stroke)	Open	2044	IM/1 mth Oral/5 mths	GPC effective
Aguglia[54] (stroke)	Open	425	IM/1 mth Oral/5 mths	GPC effective
Gambi[51] (stroke)	Open	320	IM/1 mth	GPC effective
Consoli[55] (stroke)	Open	193	IM/1 mth Oral/5 mths	GPC effective
Tomasina[56] (stroke)	Open	15	IM/1 mth Oral/5 mths	GPC effective
Mandat[52] (traumatic brain injury)	Open	23	IM/2 wks Oral/4 wks*	GPC effective

Total trials: 7   Total patients: 3040

* = Lower dose by mouth (800 mg/day) versus all other oral dosing (1200 mg/day).

Contr = controlled; DB = double-blind; PLAC = placebo; IV = intravenous (1x1000 mg/day); IM = intramuscular (1x1000 mg/day); Oral = by mouth (1200 mg/day); GPC = glycerophosphocholine

During the crucial, acute recovery phase, almost half the patients improved from being "more deteriorated" on the Mathew Scale to being "less deteriorated".[53] The physicians judged GPC had very good or good efficacy in 68% of the patients, and no or poor efficacy in 7 percent. In the second phase (oral GPC), the clinical improvement continued. All the tests gave comparable results:

- On the Mini Mental State Exam (MMSE) improvement was 12–15 percent.
- On the Global Deterioration Scale (GDS) improvement was 20 percent.
- On the Clinicians' Global Rating Scale (CGRS), improvement was 19–21 percent.

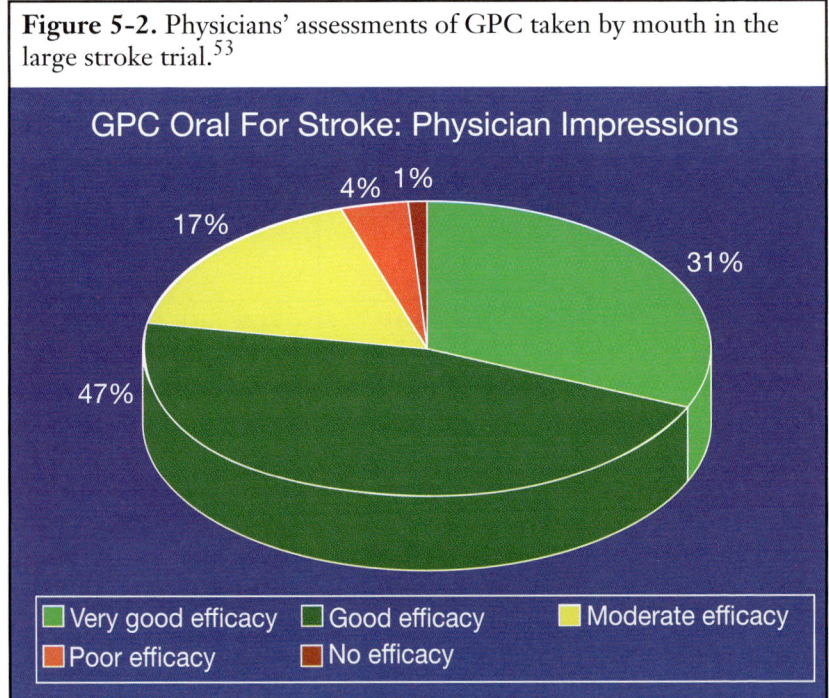

Figure 5-2. Physicians' assessments of GPC taken by mouth in the large stroke trial.[53]

The physicians judged that GPC during the oral phase had very good or good efficacy in 78% of the patients, and no or very poor efficacy in 5 percent (see Fig. 5-2).

In the 4 other stroke trials, the benefits from GPC were judged to be very similar to the huge multicenter trial (refer to Table 5-1). As with the first trial, these other clinicians concluded that intramuscular GPC in the early phase accelerated patients' recovery from the "focal neurological deficits" typical of stroke. Gambi and Onofrj, from their multicenter trial with 320 patients, praised "a considerable contraction" in the normal recovery times for stroke during the first 2 weeks of the first phase. They also stated:

> The marked resolution in 4 weeks of focal neurological deficits, particularly regarding space-time orientation, degree of consciousness, language, motor capacity and degree of invalidity…leads us to think that GPC is an optimum therapeutic choice…The changes recorded over the 5 months (of the second phase) represents an attainment of an acceptable quality of life for the patients.[51]

All the clinical research teams that conducted the 5 stroke trials were in agreement that after the first month of giving GPC i.m., GPC given by mouth gave further benefit to the patients. Professor Parnetti in her meta-analysis also clearly concluded that the clinical results suggest therapeutic effects of GPC both in the intramuscular phase and in the subsequent dietary supplement phase.[1]

By using intramuscular (i.m.) GPC the Italian clinicians may have wanted to give their very ill patients a "head start" on GPC's benefits. Or perhaps most of the patients could not swallow or keep down oral doses. GPC given i.m. does raise blood choline faster than by mouth, and to higher levels. Yet GPC taken by mouth also raises blood choline substantially, and for at least twice as long as the intramuscular injection (more than 10 hours, versus 5 hours for the injection). The patterns of choline elevation in the blood don't predict that i.m. GPC should work better over the long term than GPC as a dietary supplement.

For suitably qualified physicians who have stroke patients in their care, injectable GPC is legally available. Further data on the GPC stroke trials are provided in the Appendix. GPC is very safe to use by injection, including when given by the intravenous route.

Using GPC Toward Effective Stroke Management

Currently the options for medical management of stroke are very limited. Blood thinners may help prevent further strokes, but don't necessarily heal the damaged zones. Patients who don't make it to a hospital within 3 hours of the brain attack may not get access to these drugs.[49] Still, the stroke-damaged brain retains the potential to recover, given appropriate medical and nutritional support.

It may never be too late to begin treating a stroke. The tissue that is damaged but not dead can exist in a kind of "suspended animation". Research by Neubauer and others using hyperbaric oxygen treatment (HBOT) indicates that "stroked" brain zones can return from virtually being dead after ten years of inactivity.[57] Newer research on brain stem cells and growth factors further established that the human brain has considerable capacity to repair itself.[39,40]

Our brains possess stem cells held in reserve, mostly in the hippocampus but also scattered around the cortex. These cells have untapped potential to make new nerve cells. Our brain tissues also naturally make growth factors that support stem cell activity and overall brain adaptation (called "plasticity"). I recently reviewed the amazing advances in brain plasticity in a technical paper that appeared in the journal *Alternative Medicine Review* in December of 2005.[39] GPC supports growth factor activity in the brain, as indicated from animal experiments. GPC's role as a trophic (growth-supporting) orthomolecule will be discussed in later chapters.

While GPC's benefits for stroke are consistent, probably lifesaving in many cases, its effectiveness likely can be extended by other nutrients that have proven track records for brain support. These are PS (PhosphatidylSerine), AC (acetylcarnitine), CoQ (coenzyme Q10, ubiquinone), and RALA (R-alpha lipoic acid). These "Big Five" brain nutrients are reviewed in my 2005 *Alternative Medicine Review* paper[39] and in 2006, in a less technical 2006 article in *totalhealth* magazine.[40]

Stroke or brain attack sometimes gives an early warning. Anyone who has a "mini-stroke" or TIA is at very high risk for a big stroke in the near future (1 year or less). They would be well advised to immediately begin working with a healthcare professional to normalize their blood pressure, lose excess weight, clean up their diet, and take beneficial dietary supplements including GPC. The best way to avoid damage from a brain attack is to not have it in the first place.

Preventable Risk Factors for Stroke

There is a matrix of risk factors for stroke, just as there are for dementia (refer to Chapter 4). And as with dementia risk, control over most of the stroke risk factors is within the reach of the thinking individual. According to the American Heart Association (see *Resources*), and other sources, the most serious stroke risk factors are:

Transient Ischemic Attacks (TIAs). These are themselves near-strokes, or mini-strokes. Any TIA signals probable risk of stroke, and one that lasts more than 10 minutes is a very strong stroke predictor.[49]

High Blood Pressure (Hypertension). This is the most important controllable risk factor for stroke. In 2003, some 65 million Americans were diagnosed hypertensive—almost one third of the population. Subjects with hypertension have about twice the lifetime risk of stroke.[49] People with low blood potassium levels, and users of diuretic drugs, may be at very high risk of stroke.

Hypertension often goes undiagnosed even though it is easily detected. It has no obvious clinical symptoms or early warning signs, and that's why we all should get regular checks on our blood pressure. High blood pressure often is manageable simply through dietary and lifestyle changes and without having to use drugs.

Cigarette Smoke. Smoking approximately doubles a person's risk for stroke.[49] For women who smoke, taking birth control pills can raise stroke risk to a catastrophically high level. Also, in postmenopausal women hormone replacement using non-natural hormones also can increase stroke risk, according to the American Heart Association (see *Resources*).

Alcohol and Other "Lifestyle Drugs." Drinking an average of more than one alcoholic drink a day (women) or more than two drinks a day (men) can raise blood pressure and consequently increase risk for stroke. Cocaine use has been linked to strokes and heart attacks, some of which were fatal even in first-time users. Other intravenous drug abuse similarly elevates stroke risk.

Obesity. This condition, which often occurs together with hypertension, is now epidemic in the industrialized countries. Obesity increases the risk for just about every disease, and is a major risk factor for stroke and other brain diseases linked to poor circulation (the so-called "cerebrovascular diseases"). Physical activity helps counter obesity, and most experts advise that individuals try to get a total of at least 30 minutes of activity on most days of the week.

High Blood Cholesterol. Abnormally high *total cholesterol* in the blood is a major risk factor for heart disease, which in turn raises stroke risk. High *LDL cholesterol* and high *triglycerides* increase stroke risk in people with previous coronary heart disease, ischemic stroke or transient ischemic attack (TIA). Abnormally low *HDL cholesterol* also may raise stroke risk.

Diabetes mellitus. Having diabetes increases risk of stroke. Plus, many diabetics also have high blood pressure and high blood cholesterol, and are overweight. This increases their risk even more.

Carotid or Other Artery Disease. As with the heart's coronary arteries, when the carotid artery that supplies the brain is narrowed by atherosclerosis, the risk for "ischemic" stroke (via blood deprivation) is increased. Carotid blockage is linked to one-third to one-half of all strokes. Ultrasound can detect carotid blockage and measures can be taken to clear the blocked artery.

Patients with peripheral arterial disease (PAD) often have abnormal narrowing of the vessels carrying blood to the leg and/or arm muscles. Such patients have a higher risk of carotid artery disease, which raises their risk of stroke.

Atrial Fibrillation. People with atrial fibrillation (AF), a type of irregular heartbeat, may have a five times greater stroke risk.[49] According to a 2006 article in *The Wall Street Journal*, AF may afflict about two and a half million Americans, and has been linked to 100,000 strokes annually in the U.S. Atrial fibrillation is thought to be the leading cause of stroke among older women.

Other Stroke Risk Factors.[49] These include advancing age; coronary heart disease or heart failure; dilated cardiomyopathy (an enlarged heart); heart valve disease; and some types of congenital heart defects. Then there is sickle cell anemia, which mainly affects African Americans. "Sickled" red blood cells are less able to carry oxygen, and tend to stick to blood vessel walls, sometimes blocking arteries to the brain and causing a stroke.

CHAPTER 6

Real Benefits Against Brain Trauma

- GPC aids functional recovery following traumatic brain injury.
- GPC has been used with success to treat severe brain damage.
- GPC supports the brain's natural restorative processes.

T he brain is a delicate organ. It is easily damaged by oxygen starvation, by problems with its blood supply, by blood sugar fluctuations. The brain is especially vulnerable to these metabolic limitations because it is the most metabolically active organ. The 3-pound human brain uses at least 20 percent of all the body's oxygen and blood sugar when at rest; when it is very active this figure gets even higher.

The brain needs so much fuels that when its oxygen and other nutrient supplies are interrupted it can sustain crippling damage within minutes. This is how surgery or accidental injury can throw the brain into turmoil.

People who have suffered accidental damage to the brain, or traumatic brain injury (TBI) are a grossly neglected group. Pitifully few treatment options are available for those who—often in their prime—suffer this fate. According to a major 1998 conference sponsored by the U.S. National Institutes of Health, there are between 2.5 million and 6.5 million TBI survivors in America.

At this landmark conference it was estimated that TBI incidence in the U.S. is 100 per 100,000 persons, with 52,000 deaths per year. For many of its victims, TBI results in lifelong impairment of physical, cognitive, and psychosocial capacities. TBI places a great emotional and material burden on society as a whole.

Treatments for TBI are usually too little, too late. The injured brain is even more vulnerable than the healthy brain, and treatments that could be helpful must also be guaranteed safe so that the bad situation isn't made worse. Several published human trials indicate GPC is safe for people with TBI, and makes a real difference to their recovery (refer to Table 5-1 on page 43).

Few patients going into heart surgery are aware that they have roughly a fifty-fifty chance of coming out of it with brain damage.[50] Of those who emerge from bypass or other heart surgery with memory loss or other cognitive problems, some recover and some do not. GPC has been proven to benefit this type of TBI.

GPC Can Partially Reverse Surgical Brain Damage

Of patients who have a heart bypass, perhaps as many as 3 out of every 5 sustain "postoperative cognitive deficits".[58] They emerge from the surgery with changes in mood and personality, a tendency to mental fatigue, and disturbances of memory capacity. Some patients fully recover within days or weeks, others suffer chronic mental disability. GPC was tested on patients just out of heart bypass, in a randomized double-blind trial.

A group of clinicians in Italy identified 20 patients of both sexes, aged 45–65 years, who had measurable cognitive impairment following open-heart surgery for coronary bypass.[50] When tested following surgery, 45% of these patients (9 of the 20) showed reduced neuro-psychological performance (on the Benton Visual Retention Test, the Wechsler Memory Scale, and the Wechsler Adult Intelligence Scale). All 20 patients were then randomly assigned to two treatment groups.

The patients in one group received GPC, as one 1000 mg intravenous (i.v.) injection per day for the first month then as one 1000 mg intramuscular (i.m.) injection per day for 5 more months. The other group received a placebo i.v. for the first month, then no further treatment for the next 5 months.

By the 4 week time point, testing revealed that the patients who received GPC had memory scores significantly better than those on the placebo.[50] Over the following 5 months the placebo group continued to decline, with their memory continuing to deteriorate at the end of the 6 month trial period. The GPC group was far better off—at 6 months they had reversed their decline and were almost back to their healthy pre-surgery baseline.

Success with GPC Against Traumatic Brain Injury

GPC has been used to successfully treat a variety of traumatic brain injuries (TBI). Two clinical trials that explored GPC for TBI are discussed in the *Appendix*. This carries clinical trials summaries of GPC as an injectable nutrient and was prepared to help qualified health professionals use GPC. Treatment with injectable GPC should be conducted under the watchful eye of an experienced physician.

Traumatic brain injury, as its name suggests, features spreading destruction to broad swaths of brain tissue. In one TBI study, GPC was used to treat 23 severely injured patients.[52] Of these, 8 had acute hematoma (bleeding under the skull) with multiple hemorrhagic foci (bleeding into the brain tissue). Seven of these had been operated on with extreme urgency, the eighth operated on later. Another 6 of these patients had cerebral contusion (brain bruising) also with multiple hemorrhagic foci, and the 9 others had concussions.

This trial was not conducted double-blind, probably because these patients were too ill and all deserved positive intervention. As with the stroke treatment protocol, the GPC protocol against TBI involved a 2-phase procedure. However, for reasons that are not clear, the TBI protocol was abbreviated compared to the stroke protocol. For the first phase GPC was given i.m. over 14 days rather than 28 days. In the second phase GPC was given by mouth, but at 800 mg per day instead of 1200 mg and for just 28 days instead of 5 months.

The patients were evaluated on the internationally recognized ATS (Adult Trauma Scale) or the Karnofsky Scale immediately upon admission, then at days 1, 2, 5, and 14 following the injury, and later at 2 and 3 months following the injury. After 3 months, 22 of the 23 patients had improved. Fourteen (14) of these 22 were independent and professionally active, scoring at 90–100% on the Karnofsky Scale. Five were independent but not yet able to work (70–80% Karnofsky Scale). The last 3 required permanent care (40–60% Karnofsky). No complications from GPC were observed.

This published report is important for the severity of the cases that were treated, and for the finding that GPC worked for such badly injured patients on a less potent protocol than was used for stroke. Of course there were no "control" TBI patients to compare GPC against, but the high rate of patient response (22 of 23 patients, 96 percent) and the high rate of almost full recovery from TBI (14 of 22 patients, 64 percent), all in just 3 months, seems very unlikely to be spontaneous healing.

Can GPC Bring Patients Out of Coma?

The simple GPC molecule is very strong medicine. But strong enough to help brain-damaged patients emerge from coma? Out of Moscow's prestigious Burdenko Neurosurgical Institute, where celebrities such as Boris Yeltsin and Soviet cosmonauts are routinely treated, came a study in which GPC reportedly was successfully used to treat patients in coma from traumatic brain injuries.[59]

The Russian clinicians monitored brain bioelectrical activity in

25 of these comatose patients. They reported giving huge doses of GPC by i.v., namely 150 mg per kilogram of body weight per day from day 3 to day 14 following the head injury. Since one kilogram is 2.2 pounds, this dose of GPC is equivalent to a whopping 10.5 GRAMS of GPC for a 154-lb patient. The GPC results were compared against a control group.

Using the widely accepted Glasgow Coma Scale, the clinicians reported that GPC brought about earlier emergence from the coma state (after its third day of use, on average).[59] They also claimed that after coming out of their coma the patients had less speech impairment and more improvement from their neurological symptoms than did the control patients not treated with GPC.

The full details of this trial are not available—it was published only in summary form rather than as a full research report. Nonetheless, those details that were given carried a clear message that (1) very high doses of GPC are safe for i.v. injection, (2) that GPC can help even the most severe TBI patients: those precipitated into coma by severe head injury.

Protects Brain Injury Recovery in Animal Experiments

Laboratory rats have traditionally been used in science to develop "animal models" of brain dysfunction. Two rat models for brain damage are (1) MAM rats—injected with the toxin methylazoxymethanol (MAM) prior to birth, which retards brain development; and (2) KA rats—injected with the toxin kainic acid (KA) into the adult brain, which causes brain tissue destruction and a type of amnesia. Both the MAM and KA brain damaged rats have problems both with their cognition (memory, learning, etcetera) and with their motor functions.

GPC was found to benefit both MAM and KA rats. After receiving daily GPC injections, i.m. at 100 milligrams per kilogram per day, both sets of rats showed improved memory and learning.[60] This is a relatively high GPC dose in comparison with the usual oral dose for humans, but far lower by comparison than the doses the Russian clinicians claimed they used.[59]

Besides showing improved cognitive function from GPC, the MAM rats also showed improved "locomotor" (walking) activity. The KA rats became more resistant to developing catalepsy from haloperidol (a recognized bad side effect of this drug, one which is medically prescribed for humans). Taken together, these positive findings with the MAM and KA rat models support the human findings that GPC can protect against human brain damage.

Another useful rat brain damage model is the NBM. In the basal forebrain region of the rat (and the human) is an area called the NBM (for nucleus basalis magnocellularis). The NBM is rich in nerve circuits with cells that are cholinergic, that is, rely on acetylcholine. These also are structurally linked to the hippocampus, and to zones of the cortex also essential to learning and memory functions. In Alzheimer's patients the NBM circuits often become reduced (atrophy) or are lost altogether. Study of the rat NBM and its functional interactions with other brain zones has the potential to improve science's understanding of human dementias.

The nerve toxin ibotenic acid (IA) can be accurately injected into the rat NBM to damage this zone. Soon after the injection the NBM develops damage, and so do its cholinergic circuits that project to the forebrain cortex and to the hippocampus. Biochemically, the acetylcholine (ACh) metabolism declines in these damaged circuits. The cholinergic nerve cells that use ACh, including their fine extensions (dendrites) and their cell-to-cell contacts (synapses) have been crippled. The functional result is, not surprisingly, a deterioration in cognitive performance. The NBM brain damage model has been useful for generating specific information concerning the importance of ACh circuits for cognition.

GPC was fed to NBM rats in their drinking water, at 100 mg per kg per day for 4 weeks, beginning one day after the NBM was injected with the toxin.[61] The NBM's cholinergic circuits sustained significantly less damage. GPC gave substantial protection not just to the NBM by itself, but to its cholinergic circuits that serviced the cortex and the hippocampus.[62]

Treatment of the NBM with GPC by mouth also partially protected against the loss of ACh from the NBM circuits.[63] This experimental finding is particularly impressive, first because the doses of GPC are in a range safe for use in humans, as judged from the Burdenko study; and second, because GPC was applied only after the fact—after the NBM zone had received the toxic injection.

GPC is a Versatile Brain Protectant
From brain damage experiments with GPC, the types of experiments that could not be done with humans but were done with rats, several solid conclusions can be made:

❶ GPC gives partial protection against the brain damage caused by various nerve toxins (MAM, KA, IA). GPC rescues the cognitive functions (including memory and learning) and probably also certain motor functions.

❷ GPC protects the cholinergic circuits of the cortex and hippocampus that mainly rely on the transmitter ACh. GPC also conserved ACh metabolism in the NBM area of the basal forebrain against toxic attack.

❸ GPC can protect against brain damage when given following the toxic attack.

❹ GPC given by mouth was sufficient for this range of positive effects.

The GPC intakes in the animal experiments (usually 100 mg per kg of rat body weight per day) are about equivalent to 7 grams of GPC per day by mouth for a 150-pound human. This intake is approximately 6 times greater than the recommended oral therapeutic intake for humans (1200 mg per day), which is well within the acceptable range of differences between animal species. This makes it fair to suspect that these impressive benefits with GPC on rats could also occur in humans. Actually, GPC by mouth will enhance ACh release in the rat hippocampus at just 75 mg per kg body weight per day. This is only about 4 times the oral therapeutic intake for humans.

In summary, the diverse positive effects of GPC on brain damaged rats closely match GPC's proven—and seemingly remarkable—benefits to brain damaged humans. GPC's unique protective effects for the brain, its conservation effects and its rebuilding effects, are probably based in several distinct action mechanisms. Taken together, GPC has growth-supportive effects that facilitate brain renewal—often called *trophic effects*.

GPC May Help the Human Brain Repair Itself

In 2006, writing in the pioneering magazine *totalhealth* I published an article titled *The Human Brain Can Repair Itself*. This article was a simplified version of a professional review paper I published in 2005 in the journal *Alternative Medicine Review*. That paper was focused on neurodegenerative diseases and the potential for stem cells and growth factors to assist in their management. Refer to *Resources* for how to download both these documents. They make the case that the brain can do a lot of self-repair with help from GPC.

Figure 6-1. PET (Positron Emission Tomography) as averaged from 4 Alzheimer's patients, measuring energy generation across the brain. These patients' brains were injected with cells that secrete nerve growth factor (NGF). The 4 scans on the left were made at baseline; those on the right 6–8 months later. Color bar (center) shows more yellow and red areas in the later scans, up to 3 times more energized than other areas. From Tuszynski and others, in *Nature Medicine*.[68]

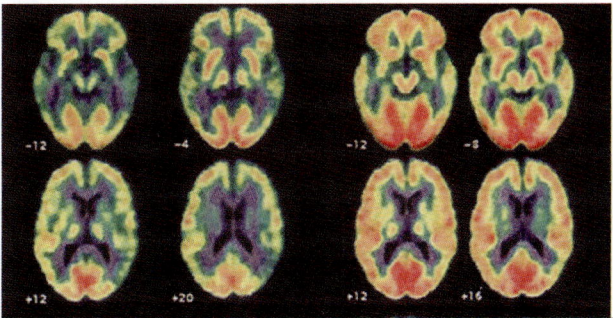

Both these publications examine the growing evidence that our human brain is capable of extensive adaptation to changing environmental inputs. That it can rebuild after it has been damaged, to some meaningful extent. That the brain decline normally associated with aging can be slowed by GPC.

Stem Cells with Growth Factors Make New Brain Circuits

Stem cells are cells that are held in reserve throughout our tissues, not yet committed to specialized functions. Stem cells have the precious capacity to make new cells to replace cells lost to injury, accumulated damage, or age. Stem cells are key to the *plasticity* of the human brain.

Plasticity is a broad term describing the brain's capacity to make adjustments to its circuitry in response to signals coming from the outside. Plasticity involves both redesigning existing circuitry, including breaking down existing synapses and making new synapses (called *synaptogenesis*);[64] and making new nerve networks (called *neurogenesis*).[65] Plasticity must be maintained with age, if the brain is to continue to adapt to life's ever-changing circumstances. And plasticity at its best requires both stem cells and growth factors.[65,66]

Growth factors for nerve tissues, technically termed neurotrophins, promote and nurture new nerve circuits.[67] Healthy brain tissue is bathed in a soup of growth factors that routinely stimulate stem cells to do ongoing cell replacement. The quality and quantity of stimuli reaching the brain affects growth factor status, which in turn affects stem cell activity.[66] In animal experiments, stimulating the learning centers typically up-regulates growth factor production and release. In turn, this intensifies stem cell conversion into mature brain cells.

Until just recently, on the basis of very old research it was generally assumed the human brain had very little plasticity. But once stem cells were discovered in the brain tissues,[65] there was a major shift in how science views the brain. Now it is clear that the human brain can do a lot more to reorganize and repair itself than was previously believed. It is likely the human brain requires intensified stimulation of the learning centers, as does the rat brain, in order to make new circuits. This gives new, practical meaning to the adage, "use it or lose it."

The first growth factor discovered is still the best studied to date. This is nerve growth factor (NGF), discovered in 1962 by Rita Levi-Montalcini, who received the Nobel Prize for this breakthrough research. Now there is direct evidence from humans, that raising NGF in the brain stimulates new circuits.

Nerve Growth Factor Can Stimulate Alzheimer Brain Regrowth

Nerve growth factor (NGF) was the first growth factor to be discovered. NGF is particularly abundant in those brain zones that are most richly endowed with cholinergic circuits. These are the circuits that rely heavily on ACh, and usually they are the first to drop out as Alzheimer's develops. Clinical researchers at the University of California at San Diego did a small experimental clinical trial on the importance of this key growth factor in the human brain.[68]

After satisfying the necessary ethical requirements for a human trial, including appropriate informed consent from the patients, the researchers injected 8 early Alzheimer's patients with each patient's own cells primed to secrete nerve growth factor. First, skin cells (fibroblasts, not stem cells) were taken from each patient, cultured using appropriate support nutrients, and implanted with a harmless virus carrying a gene for nerve growth factor (NGF). This made the skin cells able to make and release NGF. Then each patient had her/his specific cells injected into her/his own brain. The injection was targeted into the basal forebrain, the zone most often first affected by Alzheimer's.

The experiment unfortunately involved tragedy. Two patients moved their heads during the delicate brain surgery, sustained

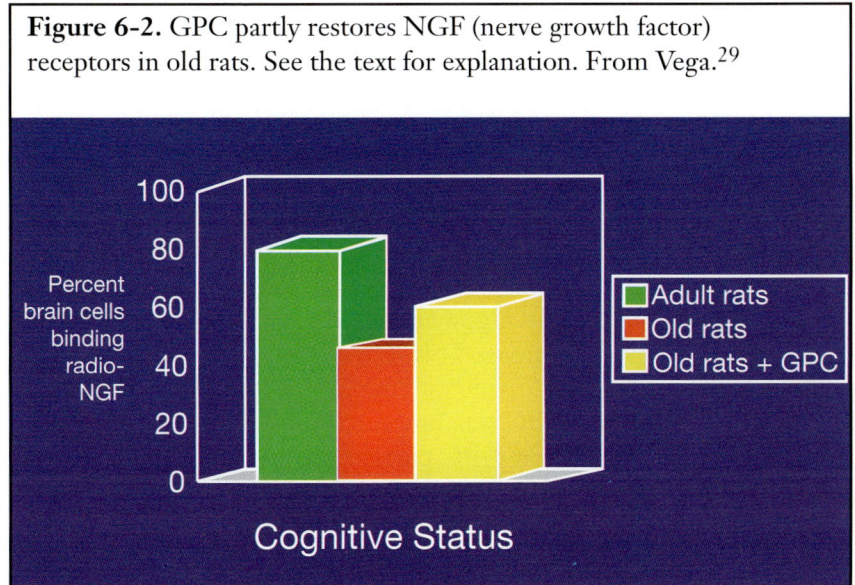

Figure 6-2. GPC partly restores NGF (nerve growth factor) receptors in old rats. See the text for explanation. From Vega.[29]

bleeding into the brain, and had to be removed from the study. One died after 5 weeks. Fine-structural examination of the forebrain from this deceased patient showed that the injected cells had indeed survived, and had released NGF. Around the zone of NGF release new nerve circuits had formed. This confirmed that the human brain, like that of the monkey and the rat, has the capacity to make brain circuits from scratch. And this in an Alzheimer's patient!

The 6 patients who remained in the study were carefully followed for 22 months. On cognitive tests and clinical assessment they showed a significant slowing of the Alzheimer's decline. Brain imaging of 4 of them (using PET, positron emission tomography, see Fig. 6-1 on page 55) showed that the cortex and cerebellum were making significantly more energy than before the operation. The plan to enhance NGF levels in the basal forebrain of these patients, achieved by transplanting their own cells primed to make NGF, indeed seemed to have worked. Structural assessments proved that new nerve cells had emerged out of the stem cell population in the basal forebrain (and very likely elsewhere in the brain), had made new nerve circuits, and had partially ameliorated the progression to dementia.

GPC Supports Nerve Growth Factor Receptor Action

Nerve growth factor (NGF) works by way of microscopic "antennas" located on the surfaces of nerve cells. Called receptors, these are implanted in the outer membrane of the cell and project out into the surrounding environment. NGF coming from outside the cell goes through a close-quarters "binding" to the receptor. This stimulates structural changes in the receptor that are transmitted through the membrane to the cell interior. The cell is then stimulated to modify its functioning in response to the NGF message. The usual response to increased NGF will be increased activity; stem cells sometimes will divide and make new cells.

In studies with rats, GPC was found to conserve the receptors for NGF. After finding that GPC partially protects the rat's cerebellar cortex against age-related decline, Vega and co-researchers decided to investigate whether GPC could up-regulate NGF receptors in that brain region.[29] They fed GPC (at 100 mg per kg body weight per day, for six months) to aged (18-month old) rats, then compared their cerebellar fine structure to adult (12-month old) rats and to aged rats not treated with GPC.

The researchers found that in the cerebellum, the Purkinje cells that carry NGF receptors and are therefore equipped to respond to NGF lessened in number between adulthood and old age. Treatment with GPC protected this cell population against aging, holding their numbers significantly higher than in age-matched rats not treated with GPC.

The numbers of NGF receptors on the Purkinje cells also significantly declined in the control aging rats, and GPC treatment cut this loss by half. The clear conclusion was that GPC extends the capacity of the aging rat brain (or more specifically, its cerebellum) to respond to NGF.

Now that it's been proven humans do have working stem cells in the brain, and that human brain growth factors can be used to generate new brain circuits, it's clear that on a practical basis the human brain can repair itself. We just have to help it along. This is where GPC comes in.

By nourishing ourselves with GPC and other nontoxic nutrients, by doing intensive mental and physical exercise, and by doing the other practices of Total Health Management, we have a real chance to revitalize our brain and achieve new levels of mind and body performance.

CHAPTER 7

How GPC Links Mind and Body

- GPC is a major body reserve for choline, a vitamin-like nutrient.
- Choline has many functions, including making AcetylCholine.
- AcetylCholine and GPC support nerve circuit renewal and repair.
- GPC also is a phospholipid reservoir for the cell membranes that support life through the body.
- GPC's many contributions to life support make it a survival nutrient.

G PC is so deeply involved in our life functions it truly can be called a survival nutrient. GPC supports a wide array of homeostatic processes that maintain the conditions necessary for life. GPC's fundamental contributions to homeostasis underlie its support for basic metabolic "housekeeping," its unique protective functions for all our cells, its rare ability to facilitate nerve circuit renewal in the damaged or aging brain.

The many life functions that GPC supports are outlined in the sections that follow.

Excellent Dietary Source of Essential Nutrient Choline

Choline is officially classified as a "dietarily essential nutrient," meaning it is practically a vitamin for humans. The Food and Nutrition Board of the Institute of Medicine at the respected U.S. National Academy of Sciences summarized the nutritional importance of choline in 1998.[69] One of their conclusions was that humans do need choline from the diet.

As with the classic vitamins, insufficient choline in the diet results in symptoms of ill-health. Over the long term, inadequate dietary choline can lead to organ dysfunction, especially liver or muscle damage.[69,70] Women with low dietary choline intake have a markedly increased risk of having a baby with neural tube defects. Choline is becoming ever more important for public health.

Choline is essential to many life processes, including those in the following categories[70]:

- A key reservoir of *methyl groups*, which are important for healthy gene regulation and numerous other biochemical and metabolic functions.
- A key source of *betaine*, another orthomolecule important for osmotic protection as well as methyl group regulation.
- Important for digestion, as a constituent of the *bile fluid.*
- Molecular building block for the mind-body messenger *acetylcholine.*
- An important backup source for the *phospholipids* PC (phosphatidylcholine) and SPH (sphingomyelin), building blocks for our cell membrane systems.

The body does make some choline internally, via "bio-synthesis". However the research suggests that this amount falls short of the total choline levels needed for good health.[69] GPC has choline naturally built into its molecular structure, is very well absorbed when taken by mouth, and is an excellent dietary source of choline. Based on the Food and Nutrition Board's recommendations, the U.S. FDA agreed to a Daily Value for choline, meaning they accept it being an essential nutrient for some humans at least. The Daily Value is currently set at 550 mg per day. This qualifies GPC as an excellent dietary source of choline. Based on the current choline DV of 550 mg per day, the intake of GPC used in most of the clinical trials would supply almost the entire choline DV (88%, to be precise).

The Basis for Choline as an Essential Nutrient

In recent years choline has become a hot topic of research. It's important for the brain at every stage of life, and especially for early brain development.[70] As the embryo develops it needs lots of choline to make and consolidate nerve circuits. Pregnant rats that consume a lot of choline have pups with greater brain power.[71] In fact, these pups tend to have superior memory and other mental performance all through their life.

As strange as this may seem, the science behind this finding is very good. And the situation may well be similar for humans. It's been known for decades that humans deprived of dietary choline develop liver problems; often these can be solved by adding more choline to the diet. Interestingly, such patients tend to score below normal on memory tests; after receiving supplemental choline their test scores significantly improved.[71]

Choline in breast milk is crucial to proper brain development after birth.[71] Yet only very little of this natural choline diet is "free" choline. Instead, the bulk of the choline in breast milk is "bound," in the form of GPC and other phospholipids.[4] This great excess of bound choline over free choline is the pattern for choline reserves all through the body. And GPC is a major body reserve for choline.

In all the body's organs and in the blood, free choline makes up only a small percentage of the total choline. Keeping most of the choline bound is probably necessary to protect against free choline doing damage. In its free form choline is so reactive that it could indiscriminately cross-react with substances not relevant to its metabolic uses. The body needs to conserve its choline and protect against wasteful loss, but have it readily accessible when needed. Using GPC fulfills these functions.

Apparently the body, in its wisdom, uses GPC as a "molecular buffer" for choline. GPC is routinely present in all the cells, and so are enzymes specialized to pull choline out of GPC.

Dr. Steven Zeisel spent many years doing the really tough research that helped choline earn the status of *essential nutrient* from the U.S. government regulators.[69–72] His research group did the major detail work that helped establish a reliable database for the choline content of various foods.[72] Topping the list of choline-rich foods are milk, liver, eggs, steak, peanut butter, oranges, and potatoes. Most of our dietary choline comes already bound, often tied up in PC or GPC.

How much choline do we need in our diet? The data available are limited, and the best guesses come out at somewhere between 500 mg and upwards of 2,000 mg (2 grams) per day.[69] Pregnant and lactating women need amounts towards the higher end of this range. People who aren't afraid to eat eggs (a very good food) or the other choline-rich foods are likely better off than the junk food consumers. Modern processing depletes the choline from our foods.

Who are the people that need to supplement with choline? Vegetarians may not get the basal intake. Pregnant and lactating women, fast growing children, sick persons, are using more choline and probably should be at the higher end of the recommended in-take range. For people who are older, there is one very good reason to take choline supplements. The brain's capacity to take choline from the blood may decline with age.

A novel technology called NMR—nuclear magnetic resonance—uses magnetic fields to conveniently measure choline in the human brain "non-invasively", without having to invade the brain tissue. Using MRI, researchers found that after taking identical doses of choline, healthy volunteers over age 65 got far less choline into their brains than did younger volunteers.

GPC is a Highly Functional Choline Source

Choline has traditionally been added to B vitamin supplements and multivitamins. The choline sources used in these supplements are pretty bad. The two most often used are choline chloride and choline bitartrate, ionic (charged) salts of choline. These are cheaper than GPC but deliver much less usable choline, milligram for milligram.

Once these ionic choline salts are taken into the mouth, they are exposed to water that liberates their free choline. Then at the intestine, much of the free choline is destroyed. Intestinal bacteria love free choline and quickly break down—most of it useless substances called trimethylamines. These are smelly and can give the body a fishy odor. In this way up to 60 percent of the choline supplement is lost to bacterial action in the intestines.

The choline salts also are technically difficult for the manufacturer to handle. Being chemically unstable, they are losing potency even as they are being manufactured into tablets or capsules. They also can pull water out of the atmosphere and ruin the other ingredients. GPC has none of these problems. It is stable during manufacture, remains stable in water, isn't degraded to trimethylamines. And being an orthomolecule, GPC is efficiently managed by the body's choline handling enzymes.

GPC does get to very high concentrations in some of our tissues. This is consistent with the great protective functions of GPC. All our cells need GPC in their water phase ("cytoplasm"), for osmotic homeostasis—GPC is an especially valuable osmotic protectant. This unique contribution of GPC is discussed in a later section.

High GPC in their cytoplasm also equips our cells for rapid response to osmotic stress, as well as for repair and growth. The choline that GPC provides is essential to gene-level control of cell activity, cell growth and cell division. In addition, enzymes present in the cells' water phase can quickly convert GPC into PC, *the* major phospholipid of all cell membranes. As cells are called upon to make new membrane mass, whether for growth or repair or expansion, they can rapidly make PC from GPC and at minimal energy cost.

Taken By Mouth, GPC Rapidly Elevates Brain Choline

Weight for weight, GPC is a rich dietary source of choline. GPC is more than 90 percent absorbed from the intestine, and about 40 percent of its weight is choline. Once absorbed into the bloodstream, GPC is rapidly circulated to all the organs and quickly taken up into the cells. GPC is an on-demand choline reserve for the body.

GPC is also an excellent "slow-release" form of dietary choline. In a "bioavailability" study done with young, healthy human volunteers, GPC taken by mouth boosted blood choline levels for more than ten hours.[73] Giving GPC by injection raises its blood levels higher than giving it by mouth, but this spike in the blood levels is back to baseline by 5–6 hours. The clinical studies done with injected GPC are summarized in the Appendix. But GPC taken by mouth as a dietary supplement gave very good clinical benefit.

From rat studies it is known that GPC by mouth does quickly get choline into the brain. Seemingly the blood-brain-barrier (BBB) lets GPC get across with little difficulty. It is suggested that specific protein transporters are available that use energy to actively draw GPC into the brain, by a process called active transport.

The BBB is a structural seal, a kind of wall, between those blood capillaries that approach the brain from the outside and those that course through the brain tissues. The BBB helps insulate the brain against potentially damaging agents. But the BBB can be counterproductive when it blocks useful substances from entering the brain. With GPC there is no such problem.

Some information is available on where GPC's choline goes after it crosses the BBB. To accurately track GPC's distribution to the brain and other organs after it is absorbed into the blood, GPC was radioactively labeled on its choline segment and fed to rats.[74] Choline was elevated in the brain a mere one-half hour after GPC was given by mouth. This helps explain how humans can feel GPC so quickly after they take it.

In this thorough bioavailability study, by 24 hours after the single GPC dose all the regions of the rat brain were enriched with labeled choline coming from GPC.[74] One observation I found fascinating was that a far greater amount of choline was localized in the pituitary than in any other brain region. The pituitary is the closest the body has to a "master gland", and the source of growth hormone. Perhaps this has something to do with GPC's impressive capacity to boost growth hormone release from the pituitary, as measured in human experiments.

An Excellent Body Reserve for AcetylCholine

AcetylCholine (ACh), is a major chemical transmitter for conveying electrical stimulation. It coordinates nerve cells with other nerve cells, in the brain and outside of it. AcetylCholine also pulls nerve cells together with muscle fibers, at nerve-muscle electrical junctions. And nerves go directly into the intestinal tract and into the various organs, where they use ACh to regulate activity in response to directions from the brain. Choline is a necessary molecular building block for making ACh.

GPC as a dietary supplement effectively raising brain choline levels, and this in turn raises production of ACh in the brain.[75] Many drugs are available for this purpose, some of them developed for Alzheimer's, but these have bad side effects that are not seen with GPC.

In experiments with rats, given GPC raised ACh in the brain, and especially in the hippocampus, the brain zone mainly responsible for creating new memories.[75] The hippocampus is heavily endowed with *cholinergic* nerve cells—nerve cells that communicate mainly using *AcetylCholine*. The cholinergic circuits of the hippocampus are directly involved with the learning process. This brain zone also happens to be the most endowed with stem cells.

The importance of GPC for the dietary support of brain ACh is seen when rats are injected with scopolamine. This chemical depletes the brain's supplies of ACh, and as a result the higher brain functions are put into suspended animation. When rats were pre-dosed with GPC, scopolamine injections failed to make them amnesic. GPC also partially protected human subjects against this scopolamine amnesia (refer to Chapter 2 for its impressive benefits to cognitive functions in these experiments).[9,10] Both these sets of experiments, with rats and with humans, prove GPC conserves brain AcetylCholine.

AcetylCholine Ties the Body to the Mind

GPC's effectiveness at elevating and conserving AcetylCholine goes beyond its choline elevating effects. Together these help explain its unique importance as a mind body nutrient for humans. AcetylCholine goes beyond other brain transmitter chemicals in the importance it has outside of the central nervous system (CNS, meaning the brain and spinal cord). Besides being important for the CNS, ACh is the main chemical messenger for the extensive networks of nerves that are located outside the CNS.[76]

Outside the CNS, ACh is the major transmitter used by the sensory nerves, by the motor nerves that drive the voluntary (skeletal) muscles, even by the nerves that connect all these.[76] Our walking, running, talking, swallowing, and other voluntary muscular movements all are driven by ACh, via the contact points between nerve endings and our voluntary or skeletal muscle fibers. These contacts are synapses, some of them very large compared to those of the brain.[77] All the nerve-muscle synapses absolutely require ACh; they cannot function without it. As a rule, the larger the synapse the more ACh is needed to keep it working.

While these functions of ACh are well recognized, its utility to the human being has another huge dimension. AcetylCholine is the most fundamental transmitter for the autonomic nervous system or ANS.[77] The ANS is a kind of automatic pilot for the body. The unconscious mind works via the ANS, using mainly ACh to manage ALL the organs of the body.

The ANS has three branches: the sympathetic, the parasympathetic, and the enteric. These operate in harmony to manage all the organs. They speed up, slow down, or hold steady the various unconscious life processes that we take for granted. The ANS maintains our vital functions—heartbeat, breathing, basic brain activity, digestion, liver and kidney functions, resistance to infection, hormones, reproduction, muscle tone, and so on—while we're awake and asleep, even while we're unconscious or in coma. And the entire ANS relies on having sufficient ACh.

AcetylCholine Also Supports Renewal of Nerve Circuits

The simple ACh molecule does more than carry messages across synapses. ACh also seems to have a growth support function.[78] That is, nerve to nerve circuits and nerve to muscle junctions seem to need ACh to grow, expand, renew, and repair damage as it occurs. In the lingo of science, this is *trophic support* and ACh is a *growth factor*. The brain growth factors or neurotrophins were introduced in Chapter 6.

For ACh to have a trophic, growth factor role means it is also important for brain plasticity. Recall from Chapter 6 that plasticity is a broad term for the brain's capacity to make adjustments to its circuitry in response to the signals coming from outside. But since cholinergic nerves are distributed to all the organs, the ACh they use is likely having trophic effects all around the body. As a reserve for the bio-synthesis of ACh, GPC makes a further contribution to mind-body integration.

The overlap of GPC and ACh as trophic factors for nerves could contribute to a synergistic trophic effect on virtually all the body's tissues. Further research is needed to investigate this possibility. If it proves real, it would give added meaning to GPC being a mind-body nutrient.

The growth factor NGF is highly involved with nerve circuits that secrete ACh. Like ACh, NGF is found widely distributed outside the brain. NGF also is a growth factor for the immune system and the endocrine (hormone system). GPC is known to support the cell surface receptors or "antennas" for NGF. Here again, by supporting NGF while backing up ACh, GPC further supports homeostasis and adaptive ("plasticity") responses all through the body.[76]

These interlocking contributions to choline, and to ACh and NGF with their widespread cholinergic and trophic effects, are evidence that GPC has premier importance for all our cells, tissues, and organs. GPC seems to be the body's preferred choline reservoir for choline, a nutrient essential to survival, growth, and freedom from disease. Choline derived from GPC also is a building block for ACh, the chemical messenger that services the tissues outside the brain. Further, ACh and NGF overlap all through the tissues. Both make important contributions to mind-body integration, and both are supported by GPC.

As if all its choline, AcetylCholine and growth factor support functions were not sufficient, the small orthomolecule GPC serves another function. GPC is a unique osmotic regulator and neutralizer of waste products.

GPC is a Unique Osmotic Protectant

As our cells are carrying out their normal life activities, they have an *osmotic pressure.* The osmotic pressure is a physical relationship between the water phase inside the cell (the cytoplasm) and the water phase outside the cell. It is a basic principle of homeostasis, that for any cell to survive it must have a neutral osmotic difference with its outside.[77]

Either positive or negative osmotic pressure is bad for the cell.

66

Figure 7-1. Proceeding from the human kidney's outer zone (cortex) to its most inner zone (papilla), GPC concentration rises in parallel with rising urea concentration.
From Wirthenson and others.[79]

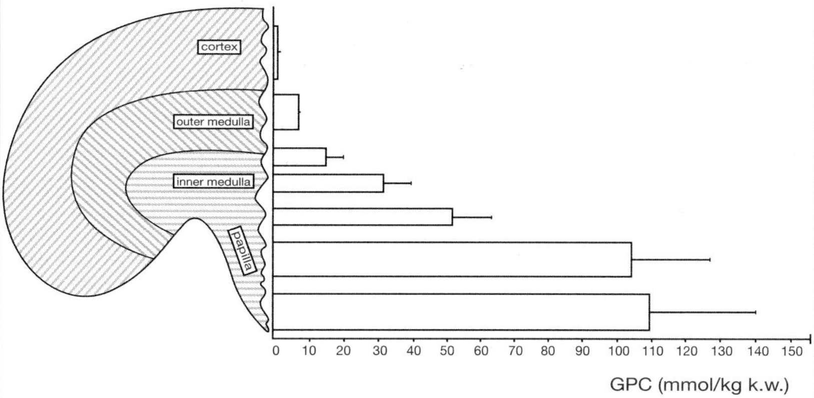

Positive osmotic pressure is when the water-phase inside the cell has more dissolved particles per unit volume than the outside. Then water is being pulled into the cell. Unless the cell can lower its osmotic pressure, water will keep coming in. The cell can expand only so far, then will burst and die, much like a balloon filling with water.

Negative osmotic pressure is when the cell's water phase has less dissolved particles per unit volume than the outside. Then water is being pulled out of the cell. Unless the cell can increase its osmotic pressure, water will keep going out. Then the cell will shrink until it no longer can function. Every cell must actively work to keep this delicate osmotic balance.

Only a very few substances are useful as *osmotic protectants*. These must be available to reach very high concentrations upon demand, at low energy cost and without becoming toxic to the cell. GPC is especially qualified in all three of these areas.[79,80]

In its role as osmotic protectant, GPC has a rare importance for all our cells, tissues, and organs. The most critical and closely studied organ system in this regard is the kidney, which routinely is subject to the greatest osmotic challenges. The kidney has the job of filtering metabolic waste products out of the blood and concentrating them into urine for eventual clearance from the body. As the urine becomes more and more concentrated, its many dissolved chemicals give it an ever higher osmotic pressure. GPC comes in very handy for the kidney, both as a general osmotic protectant and as a specific protectant against the buildup of urea.[79]

One prominent waste product in the urine is urea, from which comes the term urine. Urea becomes ever more concentrated in the urine, beginning in the kidney's cortex. As the urine fluid proceeds from the cortex into the medulla, the urea continues to become more concentrated. As the urine reaches the papilla zone that leads to the ureter, its urea levels are so high they can become toxic to the kidney cells in that zone. GPC seems to be a specific protectant against urea in the kidney.

Actually, GPC is the ONLY osmotic protectant whose concentration rises in parallel with urea in the kidney. High urea concentrations particularly threaten the proteins of the kidney cells, and GPC especially protects the cell proteins.[80] Figure 7-1 shows how the GPC concentrations inside the kidney cells rise in parallel with the increasing urea concentrations outside the cells.

Urea buildup is not restricted to the kidney, though it is most extreme there. The homeostatic use of GPC by the kidney is a clue that all our cells use GPC for defensive homeostasis. GPC protects against general osmotic damage and specifically against urea toxicity—potentially a "double whammy" attack on the cell. Having both these rare properties makes GPC an important protective orthomolecule.

Convenient Membrane Building Block for All Cells

Our staying alive depends on having good cell membranes. For more information on all the wonderful features and functions of cell membranes, consult a textbook on cell biology. My favorite is *Molecular Biology of The Cell*.[77] Here space considerations restrict the membrane story to a brief overview.

Every known type of cell, including every human cell, has its living interior separated off from the nonliving outside environment by a thin, yet continuous molecular barrier called the cell membrane. Membranes are universal to cells: From the simplest life forms to the most sophisticated, membranes are structurally the same and have a fundamental importance to life.[77] GPC is a building block for all cell membranes.

The outermost membrane, appropriately named the cell membrane, controls the access of nutrients and other agents into the cell and the release of messenger substances and waste products

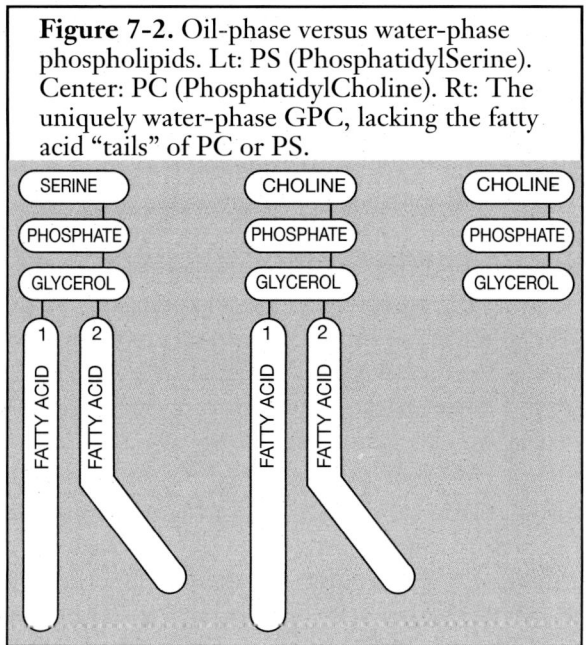

Figure 7-2. Oil-phase versus water-phase phospholipids. Lt: PS (PhosphatidylSerine). Center: PC (PhosphatidylCholine). Rt: The uniquely water-phase GPC, lacking the fatty acid "tails" of PC or PS.

from the cell to the outside. Inside the cell is a similarly organized membrane network, in which are housed most of the biochemical activities that amount to life. The outer and inner membranes are the cells' dynamic action zones.

The basic structure of all cell membranes is a "sea of lipids," a continuous molecular matrix composed mostly of two layers of phospholipids with a small contribution from cholesterol (refer to Fig. 1-2 in Chapter 1).[77] Within this matrix are arranged large protein complexes that drive the energy transformations and other biochemical—metabolic processes that support life. The matrix is composed mostly of the phospholipid PC (phosphatidylcholine), which is readily produced in the cell from GPC.[81]

As cells make new cells by dividing from one into two, in order to grow or become renewed they must make new membrane mass. This creates demand for PC, the main phospholipid that goes to make membrane mass. To make PC on demand, the most readily available and energy-efficient source is GPC.°

A Unique Water-Phase Phospholipid

As a water-phase phospholipid GPC is rare, because phospholipids are almost always located in the membrane phase. GPC in the water-phase is conveniently converted to PC, by enzymes specialized for this function. What's more, the energy needed is minimal. Therefore GPC serves to build cell membranes with very high efficiency.

Recall that the bulk of our cells' functional machinery is built into their membranes.[77] To do their basic "housekeeping" maintenance functions, to carry out their specialized responsibilities to the tissue they're in, to rebuild following damage, our cells are making new membrane mass all the time. Energy is all-important to them. GPC is an energy bargain as a source of new PC for making membrane. And once PC has become part of the membrane, other energy-efficient enzymes convert it to other phospholipids as required.

Citicoline (cytidine diphosphocholine) is also a rare water-phase phospholipid, also a resource for making PC and choline, but it is less suitable than GPC for either of these roles because it is energy-expensive. This helps explain why citicoline has been disappointing in clinical trials. Citicoline was directly compared against GPC in 3 controlled trials for treating dementia.[33-35] Citicoline proved inferior to GPC in all three.

GPC is the body's favorite, unique, water-phase phospholipid, probably because it offers special survival value. GPC is a unique protectant that can build up to huge concentrations inside our cells without doing damage. This great GPC reservoir can be drawn down at very low energy cost, to make PC for building membrane and/or to make choline and/or to help make ACh. GPC gives us a high survival "bang" for our energy buck.

Preferred Source for Omega-3 PhosphatidylCholine

Cells that are the most metabolically active have the most fluid membrane systems. Generally cell membranes are semi-liquid, but for the proteins in the membranes to move as fast as they are capable, the membrane's matrix must be close to fully liquid. This requires that many of the membrane phospholipids carry highly unsaturated fatty acids.[77] PC, as the most abundant membrane phospholipid, has to carry its share of these. Once again, Nature calls on GPC.

The GPC molecule is naturally designed for easy attachment of fatty acids, since it has none to start with (refer to Fig. 7-2). The body's favorite fatty acid for making membranes fluid is DHA (docosahexaenoic acid, omega-3). In those cells that are the most metabolically active—for example nerve cells, skeletal muscle fibers, the light-sensing cells of the retina, the spermatozoon—enzymes are in position to attach DHA molecules to GPC molecules and make DHA-PC.[81,83] As a consequence, these cells can perform their membrane functions with great speed and energy effectiveness. The clinical implications of this working alliance between GPC and DHA are profound.

Possible GPC Deficiency States in Humans

The large amount of scientific study done with GPC suggests that we humans need adequate GPC to keep our organs efficient, self-renewing, resistant to attack, and enduring over time. GPC is necessary to active living and healthy aging. The body can make GPC via bio-synthesis. But it is possible, though not yet conclusively established, that in some humans GPC is not as freely available as may be required. If we eventually confirm such cases, GPC could qualify as a conditionally essential nutrient. One GPC deficiency state has been suggested, namely Duchenne Muscular Dystrophy.[84]

Duchenne Muscular Dystrophy, Duchenne or DMD for short, is the most common muscular dystrophy in humans. It features a progressive deterioration of the voluntary muscle fibers that destroys the capacity to walk and often causes premature death. This inherited disease is based in mutation of a protein, called *dystrophin* and closely linked to the cell membrane system of the muscle fiber.[84] Analyses of skeletal muscles from Duchenne patients document a relative deficiency of GPC in those muscle fibers most affected by the disease.[85]

Infante and Huszagh[84] suggested that Duchenne might be a GPC deficiency disease. They noted that the fastest-contracting of the voluntary muscle fibers have the highest levels of DHA-PC in their membranes. This gives them the high membrane fluidity they need to rapidly transport calcium back and forth across the membrane, in and out of the fibers to make them contract then relax. The muscle fibers use GPC to make DHA-PC for their membranes.

The voluntary muscles often have mixed populations of fast and slow fibers. As a rule the faster-contracting a fiber, the more active its membrane and the higher its content of GPC and of DHA-PC. Infante and his colleague Huszagh noted that in Duchenne patients, those muscles with the least GPC are the first to break down.[84] Further research is needed, but findings as recent as 2003 support this GPC deficiency scenario as a possible factor in Duchenne Muscular Dystrophy.[85]

Supports Sperm Production and the Fertilization Process

GPC reaches extremely high levels in semen, the highest recorded concentration to date being a remarkable 100 millimolar in the ram.[86] For comparison, other small molecules very important to cell function and survival reach barely one-tenth this concentration. In human semen GPC does not reach this exceptional level. However numerous studies conducted over decades have linked low GPC in the semen to male infertility.[87,88]

The essence of spermatozoa is that they swim, strongly and for an extended period. As spermatozoa mature they become progressively enriched in DHA-PC, which results in their membranes becoming very highly fluid (see Fig. 7-3). This enables them to swim with high efficiency once the semen is ejaculated. The DHA-PC in the sperm cell most likely comes from combining DHA with GPC.81 Abnormally low GPC in the semen is linked with abnormally low sperm motility.[88]

GPC may contribute to reproductive fitness in women as well as men. Women have an enzyme in their uterine lining that breaks down GPC to make energy. After the semen with GPC has been delivered into the woman's reproductive tract, this enzyme can be released to break down the GPC into energy to help accomplish fertilization.[89]

A World of Activity in One Nutrient

Beginning decades ago, many millions of dollars were spent on clinical trials with other choline nutrients—PC, choline salts, citicoline (cytidine diphosphocholine)—for brain support and against memory decline. None of them consistently improved brain function when used as dietary supplements. But GPC works, and works well. What, then, makes GPC different from the others?

The answer to this question lies in this chapter. The answer comes from the great body of scientific findings on GPC, which together make the proof that GPC serves human health in an almost bewildering array of ways:

- As choline and acetylcholine reserve all through the body
- As nerve growth factor support, in synergy with acetylcholine
- As a rare protectant, being an osmotic regulator and urea antidote
- As a fertility support nutrient, for both men and women
- As an energy-efficient resource for cell membrane phospholipids.

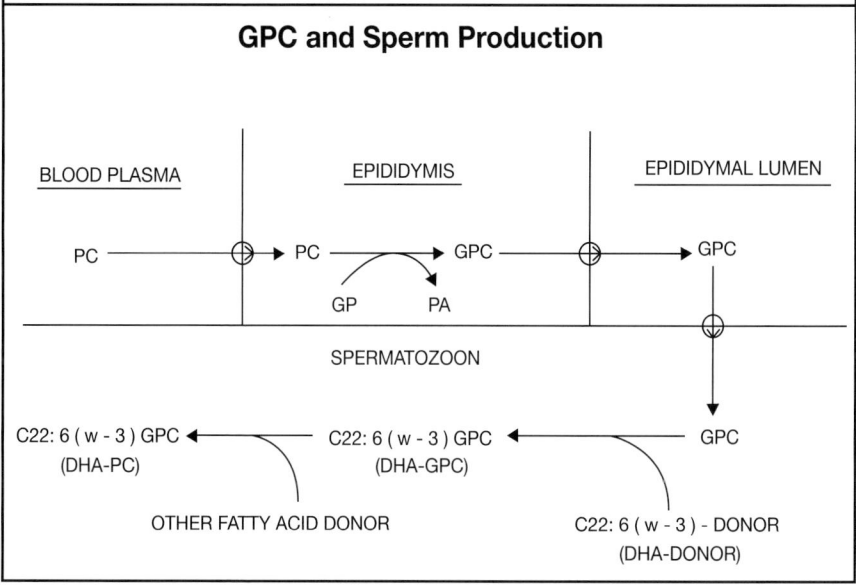

Figure 7-3. The sequence of GPC's generation and conversion to PC-DHA during sperm maturation. PC=PhosphatidylCholine, GP=GlyceroPhosphate, PA=Phosphatidic Acid, DHA=Docosahexaenoic Acid or DHA (w-3, omega-3). From Infante.[81]

So it is, then, that the vitamin-like nutrient choline, the acetyl-choline that is produced from it, and the parent molecule GPC, feed vital nerve and muscle, and other organ functions all around the body, for the good of the person as a whole. GPC is the body's natural backup for both these vital substances, and this is why I call it *a vital lipid for survival.*

GPC's value for our survival and good health is very practical because it is so safe to use. One excellent measure of the safety of GPC is the substantial amount in healthy mother's milk, consumed by the newborn baby without harm. In the clinical experience with GPC, there was no substantial risk to taking it as a dietary supplement.

The key to GPC's exceptional spectrum of health benefits is its exceptional biochemical versatility. This is what causes GPC to have multiple roles in all the cells, tissues and organs. It causes GPC to reach very high levels inside our cells, both as the unique protectant and for general metabolic support. This is what makes GPC so much more effective than the other choline nutrients, or other non-choline nutrients, or "smart" drugs. GPC is a world of activity in one nutrient.

CHAPTER 8

GPC and
Total Health Management

- GPC the nutrient orthomolecule has many "structure and function" benefits.
- GPCis safe to take and is widely compatible with other orthomolecular nutrients.
- GPC, like all nutrients, is best used along with Total Health Management™.

G PC is found almost universally in living systems, down to the simplest life forms such as Protozoa and slime molds. It's not clear whether GPC is a vitamin, because the body has the capacity to produce it. However, GPC has so many important roles for protection, growth, repair, and regulation that under stress the body's requirements for GPC could be greatly increased. If the biochemical-metabolic challenge to make GPC would be sustained, it's possible the bio-synthesis of GPC could fall behind. Then dietary GPC availability would make a difference to quality of life. This suggests GPC could be a conditionally essential nutrient.

The "Structure and Function" Claims for GPC

The 1994 Dietary Supplement Health and Education Act ("DSHEA") was a victory for freedom of choice in healthcare. It allowed for responsible claims to be made concerning a nutrient's contributions to the body's structure and function—what could also be called homeostasis. These are commonly termed structure and function claims. The following are ten such claims for GPC. From the available evidence, dietary supplementation with GPC supports:

- Attention, concentration, and recall, including in the healthy young
- Speed and sharpness of mental processing
- Positive attitude and sociability
- Recovery of brain function following circulatory deprivation
- Revitalization of declining mental function

- Metabolic efficiency throughout the body
- Growth and renewal throughout the body
- Skeletal muscle performance
- Kidney and liver performance, including detoxification
- Fertility, both sperm performance and the fertilization process

GPC as a dietary supplement is gaining a loyal following, because of what people feel when they take it, as well as from the solid science behind its use. My friend and colleague Peter Rohde, with whom I have worked on GPC for more than a decade, said this of GPC as a dietary supplement:

> GPC has four attributes that make it especially attractive to the consumer. GPC tastes good, it is fully miscible with water, it remains stable for a long time without breaking down to harmful by-products, and there's a lot of good science behind it.
>
> ∾ Peter Rohde, CEO
> Science and Ingredients Inc.
> Carlsbad, California.[90]

GPC is Safe and Well Tolerated

Though dietary supplements as a product category are far safer for humans than are pharmaceuticals, their safety cannot be taken for granted. Of the hundreds of nutrients that can be manufactured into dietary supplements, it is useful to distinguish *xenobiotic* substances (foreign to the body) from the body's intrinsic orthomolecular substances such as GPC. The xenobiotic nutrients, including those in the herbal category, are less safe than are the orthomolecules. Consistent with its orthomolecular status, GPC is a safe and well tolerated dietary supplement.

After extensive human and animal testing, GPC is proven well tolerated, non-allergenic, and safe to take long term. Commercial GPC is made from PC (phosphatidylcholine), which comes from soy. However, as with PS which is made from soy phospholipids, GPC is totally free of soy proteins or carbohydrates that could trigger soy allergy.

GPC has been proven safe in standard animal toxicology tests. In humans, after more than a decade of clinical use—including injection into more than three thousand seriously ill patients under expert supervision—GPC has shown no serious adverse side effects. The considerable clinical experience with GPC also suggests it is compatible with pharmaceuticals commonly prescribed to the elderly. Its safety and marked benefits make GPC a top nutrient for Total Health Management.

Such is the biological beauty of GPC the orthomolecule, operating in many different ways to support cell survival and metabolic "housekeeping." GPC's clean safety record and impressive clinical benefits are directly related to its broad spectrum of contributions to homeostasis.

How to Take GPC for Best Results

As a dietary supplement, GPC is usually 90 percent absorbed when taken with water between meals. The intakes used for the clinical trials was almost always 1200 mg per day, usually in divided doses: 600 mg in the morning before breakfast and 600 mg after lunch. GPC definitely extends mental endurance, and taking GPC in the evening can help a "night owl" work even later, but a clinical study found GPC did not cause insomnia.[91] For those who prefer to retire early, it is probably best to complete their GPC intake by mid to late afternoon.

For those interested in GPC for a mental tune-up, a single 600 mg dose taken in the early afternoon should be useful. For physical performance, taking 600–200 mg of GPC 2–3 hours before going on a run or to the gym will ensure that its blood levels are close to optimal during the workout. Athletic people who take GPC have made enthusiastic claims that it sharpened their physical performance.

GPC is readily compatible with most drugs and with other nutrients, with one possible exception. Persons taking *cholinergics*, drugs intended to raise brain acetylcholine levels, may want to start GPC at 300 mg daily, and increase their daily intake by another 300 mg each week, up to the maximum 1200 mg per day.

There are interesting cases of GPC benefit to children. Kids should be started on low intakes of GPC. The starting intake should probably be no more than 100 mg per day, taken preferably in the morning before breakfast. Higher intakes are likely to be safe and effective, under appropriate professional supervision.

For individuals afflicted with relatively severe brain degeneration, under medical supervision GPC can be employed via the intramuscular or intravenous routes for the first two weeks to one month, then continued by mouth long term. GPC used by itself is not a panacea, and for persons having severe problems I recommend its use in combination with other safe and effective nutrients, preferably orthomolecules.

One particularly attractive combination is GPC and PS (PhosphatidylSerine). PS is the subject of the first book in this Total Health Management series.[6] PS is a phospholipid, as is GPC, but these two nutrients exist separate from each other in the cell. PS is exclusively in the cell membrane system while GPC is not in the membranes but in the cytoplasm, the cell's water phase. While GPC is proven protective, PS is not known to be. Both are restorative, giving trophic support via NGF receptors. Both have impressive clinical records and both are safe to take.

Clinically, GPC and PS are the top two clinically proven nutrients for older people having problems with memory, mood, and the activities of daily living that keep them satisfied with life. PS is better validated for its cognitive support in healthy people over 50, while GPC is better validated for younger healthy people. Some of these apparent differences may have to do simply with different clinical research emphases. For best results, take both. At the fundamental level of the working cell, these two orthomolecular, phospholipid nutrients complement each other's actions.

Use Integrative Physicians, More Skilled With Nutrients

For people clinically diagnosed with a memory or mood disorder, I strongly recommend the use of the GPC-PS combination and other safe and effective brain nutrients as appropriate. I also recommend they find a healthcare professional committed to the integrative practice of medicine. Integrative practitioners do their very best to treating their patients as whole human beings, and put nontoxic therapies (such as nutrients) ahead of potentially toxic pharmaceuticals. You, dear reader, are encouraged to show this book to any physician.

Having an integrative practitioner on your team means you will get far better assistance with your dietary supplements and your total health management program. Amazingly, some mainstream physicians continue to have their heads in the sand and advise their patients to stop taking all vitamins! Trying to do your own self-management with only a conventional provider (the 10-minute visit) can be frustrating, ineffective, and sometimes downright dangerous to your health.

Some integrative physicians know of GPC, and many others

could use it productively in their practice. The great body of clinical findings on GPC, combined with its proven safety, motivates physicians to use GPC for patients of all ages. Taking GPC along with PS, and probably also in conjunction with DHA, should be especially helpful to optimize mental performance, to help restore functions that are out of balance, and to slow the functional decline that comes with the passing of the years.

Total Health Management Will Amplify GPC's Benefits

Most of us want to be empowered about our health. We want to stay free of disease, or to overcome our ill-health. We are aware that through our own efforts we can improve our health, and many of us are scared to death of being in a hospital. Young or old, we take our health very seriously and we pursue the Holy Grail of long life without illness.

Those of us who are working the hardest at all this are, it can be said, practicing a positive global approach to health maintenance. This I've called Total Health Management, THM for short. I introduced THM in the book on PS.[6] To practice THM is, in my opinion, the best that any of us can do to avoid sliding into a decrepit and pain-ridden life.

Practicing THM isn't easy. It means training ourselves to do good things for our health, each and every day. This doesn't mean "I can't eat anything, because the media says it's all bad for me." Nor does it mean "I can't ever have fun because I'm stuck with this stupid diet." Practicing THM means taking a deeper approach to living our daily life, with greater consciousness of what's at stake for our mind and body if we do something or if we don't.

Practicing THM also helps us avoid being misled by fatalistic watercooler talk about "bad" genes. The reality, supported by a lot of good science, is that genes have meaning and power only within the environment that surrounds them. With the full human genome now known, science is clear on this point: Unhealthy personal lifestyle, the deterioration of the modern food supply, and the polluted planetary environment, all contribute far more to our risks for catastrophic decline of brain and body than does our genetic makeup. Worrying about our ancestors' illnesses is no excuse for not practicing THM.

There's one hitch to practicing THM: it takes commitment and work. You (and I) need to really do it. This is not something that someone else can do for us, not our spouse or our doctor or our therapist. We have to be willing to listen to our body, make a commitment to staying healthy. A commitment to eating wisely, exercising regularly, meditating, getting enough sleep, thinking clearly, cultivating good judgment in personal relationships. Healthy spirit, healthy mind, healthy body. Here follow the Top Ten practices of THM.

The Top Ten Practices of Total Health Management

To empower your mind and body toward better health, master for yourself the following ten daily practices:

❶ **Avoid Toxic Agents.** Make your own list, depending on where you live and work. Begin with banning: cigarette smoke whether active or passive; excessive alcohol consumption (including beer and wine); mercury from dental fillings, vaccines, factory emissions; other heavy metals like lead, cadmium, arsenic; polluted water; pesticides, herbicides, fungicides; junk foods with rancid fats and additives; fields from high voltage power lines or cell phones; all the other known toxic factors encountered in daily living.

❷ **Use Your Brain, or Risk Losing It.** Extensive animal experimentation has shown that the more the brain is stimulated, the more it produces growth factors that help its stem cells get to work building new circuits or doing "plastic" remodeling of established circuits.[40] Those circuits that are more consistently stimulated are more likely to expand.[66] Therefore do healthy brain stimulation: take courses, play word games, card games, other games of concentration. Read good books, cut back on the television (too much TV can cause the brain to deteriorate). Memorize telephone numbers, rather than relying on automatic dialers. If you've suffered major memory loss, purchase one of the reputable memory training programs and use it every day.

❸ **Get Regular Physical Exercise.** This increases blood flow to the brain and helps the other organs as well. In animal experiments, the stem cells worked better when the animal was given a treadmill and did physical exercise.[65] Work out hard enough to break a sweat, for at least half an hour at least five times a week.

❹ **Get Rid of Emotional Stress.** This is a sadly underrated brain killer. If the reader has any doubt about how damaging emotional stress can be, read Dr. Robert Sapolsky's classic paperback *Why Zebras Don't Get Ulcers*.[45] Sometimes taking care of this problem means making hard decisions, such as to change jobs or personal relationships. Take my word for it, you'll feel a lot better when you've liberated yourself from these types of stresses.

❺ **Take Care of Your Blood Sugar.** Many life stressors, whether emotional or chemical in origin, cause you to partially lose control over your blood sugar regulation. This is particularly dangerous to the brain, which uses a big chunk of the body's blood sugar while at rest and even more of it while concentrating and doing mental tasks. Brain cells need an ongoing, smooth supply of blood glucose, and when deprived will begin to die off within minutes. If you have this problem take a hard look at your diet, exercise more and seek professional help if necessary.

❻ **Eat Sensibly and Regularly,** to keep the mind and body continually supplied with the steady supply of blood glucose and other nutrients that it needs. Buy organic foods. Eliminate refined sugar from your diet. Keep frying to a minimum—it generates harmful free radicals. Help guard against life's many free radical challenges by cooking with spices rich in antioxidants, such as garlic, onions, ginger, curry, rosemary. Seek out antioxidant foods such as berries and red and yellow vegetables. Consume more dark green leafy veggies, complex carbohydrates high in fiber, free range meats.

❼ **Be Careful of Food Additives.** Some food additives are "excitotoxins" that can drive nerve cells into a death frenzy. Glutamate, as in MSG (monosodium glutamate); and aspartate, as in Aspartame, may well be in this category. Artificial colorants are mostly suspect carcinogens. Trans-fats ("hydrogenated fats") are hidden in many foods and are linked to chronic disease. Try to stay with fresh foods that are minimally processed and packaged. Organic foods cost more but they're worth it.

❽ **Drop the Drug Lifestyle.** This includes marijuana, ALL the illegal drugs, and many of the legally available pharmaceutical drugs, are brain toxins. Cocaine, amphetamines, Ecstasy and other psychedelics, all kill brain cells, as can marijuana. Some pharmaceuticals are likely as toxic to the brain as the worst illegal drugs. This is another medical scandal waiting to happen—check the fine print.

Many drugs currently in wide use as sleep aids, as antidepressants, or for other indications, can have profound negative effects on the brain. Drugs such as Librium, Valium, Halcion, Prozac, Haldol, Xanax, Compazine, Stelazine, Thorazine and barbiturates are responsible for an estimated 10 percent of all cases that present as dementia.[43] Some of the patients fortunate enough to be taken off the drug will recover their minds.

Some of these drugs also are linked to homicidal and suicidal behavior. Sadly, many physicians prescribe drugs without being familiar with their side effects. It's up to the consumer to beware. *Worst Pills, Best Pills* is an indispensable resource for this type of information.[43]

❾ Develop Your Personal Dietary Supplement Program.
Even the most conservative physicians and scientists now agree that dietary supplements are essential for good health. Partly this is because of the lousy state of the food supply. Also, the emotional and physical stressors of modern living increase our metabolic needs for nutrients. Then, as we get older (past 40, that is) we digest, absorb, and assimilate our foods with less efficiency. My article *"Why You Should Take Vitamins,"* originally published in *totalhealth* magazine, will help you set up your own program (see the Resources section for how to contact *totalhealth* magazine). My Website has many other articles on various disorders and diseases, and nutritional protocols for each.

❿ Take Time to Sleep. This could be the most neglected part of modern life. The body needs 7 to 8 hours of sleep to renew all the tissues, including those of the brain. The brain's pineal and pituitary glands keep the body on a 24-hour schedule, synchronized according to sleep patterns. When sleep is incomplete these sophisticated hormonal cycles become disrupted, resulting in accelerated aging and greater susceptibility to disease. Try to get on a natural sleep cycle that gives you sufficient deep, restful sleep without the use of an alarm.

CHAPTER 9

GPC Has Something for Everyone

- GPC has vital benefits for people of all ages, even children.
- GPC links the mind with the body for active living and healthy aging.
- GPC is a breakthrough survival nutrient, from youth to old age.

G PC has something to offer everyone. It is that rare dietary supplement that everyone can feel soon after they start taking it. It has documented benefits for people of all ages (even children, as we shall see). GPC is truly a survival nutrient, a vital lipid that supports a wide array of life processes on which we rely to stay healthy.

In many well-controlled clinical trials, GPC improved mental performance in the healthy young, the middle-aged, and the elderly. In the trials GPC worked better and faster than several other nutrients and drugs, when directly matched against them. GPC proved superior to the drugs oxiracetam, aniracetam, and idebenone and the nutrients acetylcarnitine and citicoline. GPC's capacity to boost growth hormone release gives it an even higher level of importance.

Animal experiments suggest GPC can (at least partially) restore structure and function to the damaged brain. GPC is not a panacea, but when employed as part of Total Health Management™ (THM) it can make a great difference to the brain, mind, and body. Intrinsic to the THM survival strategy is to use all nutrients that can safely offer benefit. My intensive monitoring of the published clinical trials and related studies led me to group together GPC, PS (PhosphatidylSerine) and AC (AcetylCarnitine) as the Big Three Brain Nutrients.[39,40]

Chapter 2 described how GPC sharpens brain functions in young, healthy people. This research was done under carefully controlled, "double-blind" trial conditions. Individual reports are much less strong than double-blind trials, but when such reports keep coming we can begin to suspect that there is something to them. One consistent report is that GPC "slows the ball down."

For Active Living, GPC "Slows the Ball Down"

Racquetball is one of the most challenging games for mind and body. The racquetball player has to stay at a high level of mental focus all through the game, has to physically drive their body to locate the ball, track its movement, and target it with great precision. He or she must always be anticipating what the opponent will do next. And always the ball is moving very fast.

One friend of mine has been using GPC every time he goes to play racquetball. He is a very strong player, and he is strongly convinced GPC makes him even better. He takes a full dose of GPC (1200 milligrams) 1–2 hours before the game. During the game, he says, GPC slows the ball down. Taking GPC before the game helps him track the ball better, get to the ball faster, hit the ball harder and with greater accuracy.

Other friends who play less demanding physical games have related favorable experiences with GPC. You don't have to believe them. But you may want to try it yourself, for whatever physical, mental, or mind-body calisthenics you like to do.

Early on, soon after I helped introduce GPC into north America, I got several reports from male friends that GPC might be having revitalizing effects on certain of their especially valuable organ systems. They wouldn't tell me exactly which organ systems it seemed to help the most.

When I take GPC, my mental endurance seems to increase. I keep pounding away at my keyboard, or get to reading technical scientific papers, and tend to lose track of the time. GPC extends my mental endurance, allowing me to stay mentally focused for longer periods of time.

None of these musings can be called scientific, but science can't always measure subtle and individual benefits from a nutrient. I urge you, dear reader, to try GPC for yourself.

A Survival Nutrient for Healthy Aging

GPC supports brain survival, literally. In the 5 trials conducted with stroke survivors, the 3 trials with traumatic brain injury patients, and the double-blind trial on patients cognitively damaged by heart bypass surgery (refer to Table 5-1 and the Appendix), GPC produced clinically remarkable improvement and was well tolerated.

In no less than 12 trials on dementia, the majority of them randomized and controlled, GPC proved its worth at slowing brain decline (refer to Table 4-1). GPC's benefits for this patient population surpassed the "smart drugs" aniracetam and oxiracetam, the drug idebenone, and nutrients acetylcarnitine and citicoline.

GPC is particularly unique for its protective properties. As an osmotic buffer GPC helps the kidney cells (and all the body's other cells) avoid destruction. With its rare zwitterionic chemical structure (having a positive and a negative charge on the same molecule), GPC is especially suited for buffering the cell cytoplasm against metabolic problems.

From the large body of research on GPC's metabolism it appears that the body uses GPC for general stability through homeostasis, and specifically to cope with stresses such as urea buildup and to facilitate normal maintenance, growth, and repair. All at minimal energy cost. Our cells have a feedback mechanism that shuts down GPC breakdown, to conserve GPC and keep it available for use as necessary.[92] This may be the means by which GPC levels rise in damaged brain tissues.

As GPC builds up in the damaged brain, its higher concentration would tend to drive reactions converting it to the phospholipid PC. This PC would be needed to make new membrane mass for repair, and to rebuild lost connections. Interestingly, GPC's relative GPE (glycerophosphoethanolamine) also tends to accumulate in damaged nerve cells. This also would encourage new cell membrane assembly, since PC and PE are the most common phospholipids of membranes.

Likely Value for Autistic Children

Childhood autism is a complex disorder that displays malformation of nerve circuits in the brain's cortex, hippocampus and other regions. A group at the Russian Academy of Medical Sciences' Mental Health Science Center explored GPC's benefits for autistic children.[93]

These clinicians recruited 20 children (16 boys, 4 girls) aged from 3 to 8 years, into an open (non-randomized, non-blinded) trial. The children were allowed to stay on the pharmaceuticals they had been taking prior to the trial. The starting intake of GPC was 400 mg, once a day before breakfast. The researchers soon realized that for some children this intake was too much, and reduced it to 400 mg every other day. All the children completed 4 weeks on GPC, and at the trial's end (8 weeks) 15 of them were still taking GPC.

The children who stayed on GPC all the way through the study seemed to derive meaningful benefit from it. The researchers judged that none of them showed clinical decline while on GPC, and that 89% showed minimal to significant improvement. The majority of the children were judged improved in many different aspects of behavior, mood and cognition. According to the clinicians:

● The patients began to make attempts to interact with other children and to take part in group, chiefly motor, games…Fear of the arrival of unfamiliar adults and children into the home and refusal to visit new places vanished…The emotional sphere livened up…The children began to display emotional interest in their mothers.

● Improvement in communicative skills was manifested as…appearance of more prolonged eye contact and emotional response… A change was also noted in speech development. Comprehension of speech improved. Children who could talk began to talk more…In cases where expressive speech was lacking, there was an appearance of syllabic speech…

● Understanding, consideration of surroundings, self-restraint, and the ability to alter behavior appeared…the children stayed restrained in class longer and followed orders without the need for repetition several times…

● Mood improved…the children became more cheerful…Negativism diminished significantly, even in patients with severe persistent negativism which had not responded to previous therapy.

● A significant increase in cognitive ability was also noted…Concentration of attention on assigned tasks improved…Lapses into fantasy and autistic introversion occurred considerably less often.

● Improvement was also noted in motor development…in fine motor skills and personal care skills…they mastered skills whose formation required comprehending a series of necessary actions.

The findings from the various objective scoring scales confirmed the subjective impressions of improvements in social skills, communication skills, speech, personal care, obstinacy and aggressiveness, mood, productive activity, and motor functions. The researchers recommended GPC "as an effective and safe means of treating cognitive and behavioral disorders in patients with mild and moderately severe childhood autism."

GPC, Mind-Body Nutrient From Youth to Old Age

The considerable clinical and other scientific data on GPC suggest that for us humans, it is nothing less than a survival nutrient. Its production in all our cells is under sensitive control and its levels can be increased as necessary. It serves the entire body as a reserve for many vital biomolecules. Its conversion to other molecules is rapid and energy efficient. GPC is also a vital protective orthomolecule that attains unprecedented high levels in some of our cells, tissues and organs. GPC is a vital lipid for survival.

GPC's fundamental importance to life is apparent from its relative abundance in mother's milk. The generational transition—from fertilization through to birth and after—depends on sufficiency of GPC for making PC-DHA for the sperm and fertilization, for choline to support brain formation *in utero*, as well as for acetylcholine and other substances essential to early childhood development.

GPC's wide range of involvements in our life processes makes it important from the cradle to old age. Yet we cannot count on ample supplies of it from the modern diet, so that taking GPC supplements is a means of nutritional life insurance. GPC's use as a safe and effective injectable for badly hurt patients adds further meaning to the concept of nutritional life insurance (see the Appendix).

For some people with severe health burdens, GPC could be a lifesaver. For patients afflicted with stroke, the memory loss and other cognitive problems that often follow surgery, or traumatic head injury, GPC offers safe and effective intervention to salvage quality of life if not life itself. Its evident promise as a growth hormone releaser and possible pituitary gland revitalizer, as seen in three clinical experiments, deserves to be more fully explored.

GPC is a mind-body nutrient without equal. GPC supports the mind by boosting the brain's all-around performance. It supports the body by way of its protective and other biochemical support for all the organs. It supports physical performance by providing choline for the acetylcholine that drives the skeletal muscles and the autonomic nervous system. Indeed, by its all-around support for homeostasis of mind and body, GPC supports virtually all of active living.

Most of us wish for active living well into old age. We hope to navigate the aging process with freedom from crippling disease. GPC may not be an "anti-aging" panacea, but it does offer proven nutritional support for healthy aging of all the organs.

GPC is a safe and effective dietary supplement that offers us a chance for active living in our youth, and for continued integrity of mind and body as we age. I urge you, dear Reader, to empower your health with the help of GPC.

Resources

Alzheimer's Association (U.S.) Website, www.alz.org Authoritative source of statistics on Alzheimer's and other dementias, with information also on pharmaceuticals approved or under investigation.

Alzheimer's Prevention Foundation International, Tucson, Arizona, tel 520-749-8374, www.alzheimersprevention.org Founded by Dharma Singh Khalsa, M.D. Currently the most comprehensive program available for reversing mental decline.

Amen, D.G. *Images of Human Behavior. A Brain SPECT Atlas.* Newport Beach, California: MindWorks Press, 2003. www.mindworkspress.com A dazzling collection of images of healthy, damaged, or diseased brains obtained via metabolic SPECT imaging in the clinics of Daniel Amen, M.D. A must-see for the serious brain student or parent of a troubled child.

American Stroke Association, www.strokeassociation.org Valuable information on stroke, including signs, emergency treatment, statistics on incidence and survival.

Crook T, Adderly B. *PS, The Memory Cure.* New York: Pocket Books, 1998. Dr. Tom Crook, world expert on cognition testing and age-associated memory impairment, co-wrote this very nice book. In it he presents a 6-step plan for sharpening mental skills.

Khalsa, D.S. and Stauth, C. *Brain Longevity: The Breakthrough Medical Program.* New York: Pocket Books, 2001. Now a classic in the field. Available from the Alzheimer's Prevention Foundation International, tel 520-749-8374, www.alzheimersprevention.org

Khalsa, D.S. and Stauth, C. *Meditation as Medicine.* New York: Pocket Books, 2001. Another pioneering work by this cutting-edge brain healer. Barnes and Noble health book of the year. Available from the Alzheimer's Prevention Foundation International, tel 520-749-8374, www.alzheimersprevention.org

Khalsa, D.S. *The Better Memory Kit,* 2004. Alzheimer's Prevention Foundation International, tel 520-749-8374, www.alzheimersprevention.org

Kidd, P.M. *PS (PhosphatidylSerine), Nature's Brain Booster for Memory,* Mood and Stress (Total Health Management Series No. 1). St. George, Utah: Total Health Communications, tel 435-673-1789, www.totalhealthmagazine.com An overview with full documentation of another phospholipid nutrient that complements GPC as one of Dr. Kidd's Big Three Brain Nutrients.

Kidd, Dr. Parris Website, www.dockidd.com Wide array of articles for lay people, scientists and physicians on integrative management of memory decline, dementia, ADHD, autism, bipolar disorder, Parkinson's, multiple sclerosis, and less common brain disorders. Also Dr. Kidd's columns from *totalhealth* magazine.

Passwater, Richard, Ph.D. www.drpasswater.com Nutrition pioneer, prolific author, contributor to the development and application of dietary supplements for more than 3 decades. His Website lists his 40 books and much more.

Perlmutter, David, M.D. Website, www.BrainRecovery.com Brilliant integrative physician tackling the most difficult to treat brain conditions. His classic book *Brain Recovery.com* carries indispensable information and treatment protocols. His recent *The Better Brain Book* (authored with Carol Colman) expands on his earlier protocols and includes newer diagnostic tests and cooking recipes.

Phospholipid Educational Website, www.phospholipidsonline.com Covering phospholipid types and applications, with the participation of Dr. Parris Kidd.

Rapp, Doris, M.D., www.drrapp.com A physician who has dedicated her career to identifying and eliminating toxic influences on the human environment from foods and pollutants. Her latest book, ***Our Toxic World: A Wake-Up Call,*** should be in the home of every family.

Smith, Dr. Kyl, www.BrighterMind.com, brain expert and author of ***Brighter Mind,*** a comprehensive book that covers "the foods to eat for the brain, the nutrients to take, the exercises and activities to do, in order to experience maximal brain performance at every age."

totalhealth magazine, published by Total Health Communications, St. George, Utah, tel 435-673-1789, www.totalhealthmagazine.com The nation's foremost magazine promoting citizen empowerment in health management.

U.S. Food and Drug Administration (FDA) Center for Food Safety and Applied Nutrition, www.cfsan.fda.gov Official regulatory documents for the U.S. government's positions on dietary supplements.

U.S. National Institutes of Mental Health (NIMH), www.nimh.nih. gov/health information. Conservative but responsible source for information on ADHD, autism, bipolar disorder, major depression, and other mental illness.

Worst Pills, Best Pills II, www.citizen.org/publications Published by Dr. Sidney Wolfe and the Public Citizen Health Research Group, Washington, DC. An honest, uncorrupted reference for pharmaceuticals in common use or recently developed for use. Encyclopedic and affordable, a must reference for every home.

Scientific References in the Text

1. Parnetti L, Amenta F, Gallai V. Choline alfoscerate in cognitive decline and in acute cerebrovascular disease:an analysis of published clinical data. Mechanisms of Ageing and Development 2001;22:2041–55.
2. Pauling L. Orthomolecular psychiatry. Science 1968;160:265–73.
3. Kunin R. Orthomolecular medicine-personal communication. San Francisco, California: Private practice;2002.
4. Holmes-McNary M and others. Choline and choline esters in human and rat milk and in infant formulas. Am. J. Clin. Nutrition 1996;64:572–6.
5. Kidd PM. Dietary Phospholipids as Anti-Aging Nutraceuticals. In, Anti-Aging Medical Therapeutics, Vol. IV, ed. Klatz RA, Goldman R. Chicago, IL: Health Quest Publications; 2000.
6. Kidd PM. PS (PhosphatidylSerine), Nature's Brain Booster for Memory, Mood, and Stress. St. George, UT, USA:Total Health Communications;2005.
7. Bluml S, Seymour KJ, Ross BD. Developmental changes in choline-and ethanolamine containing compounds measured with proton-decoupled 31P MRS in *in vivo* human brain. Mag. Reson. Medicine 1999;42:643–54.
8. *totalhealth* magazine. St. George, UT, USA: Total Health Communications, tel 888.316.6051; totalhealthmagazine.com
9. Canal N, Franceschi M, Alberoni M and others. Effect of L-a-glyceryl-phosphorylcholine on amnesia caused by scopolamine. Intl J. Clin. Pharmacol. Ther. Toxicology 1991;29:103–7.
10. Canal N, Alberoni, M, Bressi, S and others. Comparison of the effects of pretreatment with choline alfoscerate, idebenone, aniracetam and placebo on scopolamine-induced amnesia. Le Basi Raz. Terapia 1993;23:102–7.
11. Wesnes K, Simpson P, Kidd A. An investigation of the range of cognitive impairments induced by scopolamine. Hum. Psychopharmacology 1988;3:27–41.
12. Govoni S, Lopez CM, Battaini F and others. Chronic treatment with an acetylcholine synthesis precursor, alpha-glycerylphosphosphorylcholine, alters brain parameters linked to cholinergic transmission and passive avoidance behavior. Drug Dev. Research 1992;26:439–47.
13. Schettini G, Ventra C, Florio T and others. Molecular Mechanisms Mediating the Effects of L-a-glycerylphosphorylcholine, a new cognition-enhancing drug, on behavioral and biochemical parameters in young and aged rats. Pharmacol. Biochem. Behavior 1992;43:139–51.
14. Lopez CM, Govoni, S, Battaini F and others. Effect of a new cognition enhancer, alpha-glycerylphosphorylcholine, on scopolamine-induced amnesia and brain acetylch line. Pharmacol. Biochem. Behavior 1991;39:835–40.
15. Imperato A, Casolini P, Patacchioli FR and others. Brain utilization of choline-alfoscerate: a microdialytic study. Neurosci. Letters (Suppl.) 1990;39: s119.
16. Moglia A, Bergonzoli S, De Moliner P. Effect of a-GFC in brain mapping changes in patients with age associated memory impairment (AAMI). Le Basi Raz. Terapia 1990;20:83–9.
17. Sannita WG. Techniques of functional exploration of the SNC and models of cholinergic functioning. Le Basi Raz. Terapia 1993;23:81–9.
18. Lacomba C, Cagiano R, Maci O and others. Effects of L-alpha-glycerylphosphorylcholine on the EEG power spectrum in the rat. Drug Dev. Research 1992;26:101–7.
19. Abbati C, Rondi G, Rosola R and others. Nootropic therapy of cerebral aging. Adv. Therapy 1991;8:268–75.
20. Vezzetti V, Bettini R. Clinical and instrument evaluation of the effect of choline alfoscerate on cerebral decline. La Presse Medicale 1992;5:141–4.
21. Sicurella L, Mattina G, Santagati A and others. Changes in VEP in subjects treated with alphaGFC. Preliminary study. Le Basi Raz. Terapia 1990;20(3 Suppl. 1):91–3.
22. Klatz R, Kahn C. Grow Young With HGH. New York: Harper Collins; 1997.
23. Corpas E and others. Human growth hormone and human aging. Endocrinol. Reviews 1993;14:20–8.

24. Ceda GP, Ceresini G, Denti L and others. Alpha-Glycerylphosphorylcholine Administration Increases the GH Responses to GHRH of Young and Elderly Subjects. Horm. Metab. Research 1991;24:119–21.

25. Ceda GP, Marzani GP, Tontodonati V and others. Effects of an acetylcholine precursor on GH secretion in elderly subjects. In, Growth Hormone II: Basic and Clinical Aspects, ed. Bercu BB, Walker RF. New York: Springer-Verlag; 1994, 328–37.

26. Schettini G and others. Effect of choline alfoscerate in elderly patients with primary degenerative dementia. Le Basi Raz. Terapia 1993;23 (Suppl. 3):108–16.

27. Amenta F, Bronzetti E, Mancini M and others. Choline acetyltranferase and acetylcho linesterase in the hippocampus of aged rats: sensitivity to choline alphoscerate treatment. Mechs. Ageing Development 1994;74:47–58.

28. Amenta F, Liu A, Zeng Y and others. Muscarinic cholinergic receptors in the hippocampus of aged rats: influence of choline alphoscerate treatment. Mechs. Ageing Development 1994;76:49–64.

29. Vega JA, Cavallotti C, Del Valle ME and others. Nerve growth factor receptor immuno reactivity in the cerebellar cortex of aged rats: effect of choline alfoscerate treatment. Mechs. Ageing Development 1993;69:119–27.

30. De Jesus Moreno Moreno M. Cognitive improvement in mild to moderate Alzheimer's dementia after treatment with the acetylcholine precursor choline alfoscerate: a multi center, double-blind, randomized, placebo-controlled trial. Clin. Therapeutics 2002;25:178–93.

31. Paciaroni E, Tomassini PF. Clinical study of effectiveness and tolerability of alpha-GFC (choline alfoscerate) vs. oxiracetam in patients suffering from slight/moderate cognitive defect of vascular origin. G. Ital. Rech. Clin. Terapeutiche 1993;14:29–34.

32. Parnetti L, Abate G, Bartorelli L and others. Multicentre study of l-a-glyceryl-phosphor ylcholine vs ST200 among patients with probable senile dementia of Alzheimer's type. Drugs and Aging 1993;3:159–64.

33. Frattola L, Piolti R, Bassi S and others. Multicenter clinical comparison of the effects of choline alfoscerate and cytidine diphosphocholine in the treatment of multi-infarct dementia. Curr. Ther. Research 1991;49:683–93.

34. Di Perri R, Coppola G, Ambrosio LA and others. A multicentre trial to evaluate the efficacy and tolerability of a-glycerylphosphorylcholine versus cytosine diphosphocholine in patients with vascular dementia. J. Intl Med. Research 1991;19:330–41.

35. Muratorio A and others. A neurotropic approach to the treatment of multi-infarct dementia using L-a-glycerylphosphorylcholine. Curr. Ther. Research 1992;52:741–52.

36. Ban TA, Panzarasa RM, Borra S and others. Choline alfoscerate in elderly patients with cognitive decline due to dementing illness. New Trends Clin. Neuropharmacology 1991;5(3/4):87–121.

37. Palleschi M, Zuccaro SM, Rubegni M and others. Evaluation of effectiveness and tolerability of alpha-GFC (choline alfoscerate) in patients suffering from slight/moderate cognitive decline. Preliminary results. Geriatria 1992;4:13–20.

38. Bassi S, Albizzati MG, Piolti R and others. Clinical experience with choline alphoscerate in patients affected by degenerative and multi-infarct dementia. Gnosis 1990;5:55–62.

39. Kidd PM. Neurodegeneration from mitochondrial insufficiency: stem cells, growth factors, and prospects for brain rebuilding using integrative management. Alt. Med. Review 2005;10:268–93.

40. Kidd PM. The human brain can repair itself: stem cells, growth factors, and brain nutrients. totalhealth magazine, Mar/Apr 2006.

41. Kidd PM. A review of nutrients and botanicals in the integrative management of cognitive dysfunction. Alt. Med. Review 1999;4:144–61.

42. Tierney MC, Szalai JP, Snow WG and others. A prospective study of the clinical utility of ApoE genotype in the prediction of outcome in patients with memory impairment. Neurology 1996;46:149–54.

43. Wolfe SM and the Group. Worst Pills, Best Pills II. Washington, D.C., USA: Public Citizen Health Research Group; 1993.

44. Lupien S, de Leon M, de Santi S and others. Cortisol levels during human aging predict hippocampal atrophy and memory deficits. Nature Neuroscience 1998;1:69–73.
45. Sapolsky RM. Why Zebras Don't Get Ulcers: A Guide to Stress, Stress-Related Diseases, and Coping. New York, NY, USA: W.H. Freeman; 1994.
46. Rapp DJ. Our Toxic World. Buffalo, NY, USA: Environmental Medicine Research Foundation; 2004.
47. Amen DG. Images of Human Behavior. A Brain SPECT Atlas. Newport Beach, CA, USA: MindWorks Press; 2003.
48. Geula C, Mesulam MM. Cortical cholinergic fibers in aging and Alzheimer's disease: a morphometric study. Neuroscience 1989;33:469–81.
49. Thom T, Haase N, Rosamond W and others. AHA Statistical Update: Heart disease and stroke statistics-2006 update (American Heart Association). Circulation. 2006;113:e85–e151.
50. Auteri A, Bova F, Chiarion C and others. Protecting the brain during heart surgery: treatment with choline alfoscerate. Le Basi Raz. Terapia 1993;23:123–8.
51. Gambi D, Onofrj M. Multicenter clinical study of efficacy and tolerability of choline alfoscerate in patients with deficits in higher mental function arising after an acute ischemic cerebrovascular attack. Geriatria 1994;6:91–8.
52. Mandat T, Wilk A, Monowiec R and others. Preliminary evaluation of risk and effectiveness of early choline alphoscerate treatment in craniocerebral injury. Neurol. Neurochirurgia 2003;37:1231–8.
53. Barbagallo Sangiorgi G, Barbagallo M, Giordano M and others. alpha-Glycerophos phocholine in the mental recovery of cerebral ischemic attacks. Ann. N. Y. Acad. Sciences 1994;717:253–69.
54. Agnglia F. and others. Choline alphoscerate in the treatment of mental pathology following acute cerebrovascular accident. Funct. Neurology 1993;8 (Suppl):5–24.
55. Consoli D, Giunta V, Grillo G and others. Alpha-GPC in the treatment of acute cerebro-vascular accident patients [translated from the Italian]. Arch. Med. Interna 1993;45:13–23.
56. Tomasina C, Manzino M, Novello P and others. Clinical study of the therapeutic effectiveness and tolerability of choline alfoscerate in 15 subjects with compromised cognitive functions subsequent to acute focal cerebral ischemia. Riv. Neuropsichiatr. Sci. Affini 1996;37:21–8.
57. Neubauer RA, Gottlieb SF. Hyperbaric oxygen, idling neurons, and stroke management (letter). J Crit. Illness 1993;8(8):15.
58. Boodhwani M, Rubens FD, Wozny D and others. Predictors of early neurocognitive deficits in low-risk patients undergoing on-pump coronary artery bypass surgery. Circulation 2006;114 (1 Suppl):I461–6.
59. Madorskyi S, Amcheslavskyi V. L-a glicerylphosphoryllcholin in treatment of consciousness disorders after head injury. Neuropsychopharmacology 1994;10 (3S, pt 2):8S (abstract only).
60. Genazzani AA, Grassi M, D'Agata V and others. Behavioral effects of a-GFC in patho-logical brain aging models. Neurosci. Letters 1990;supp 39:s100.
61. Ciriaco E, Bronzetti E, Ricci A and others. Influence of ipsilateral lesions of the nucleus basalis magnocellularis and of choline alphoscerate treatment on histochemically reactive zinc stores and on the ultrastructure of the rat frontal cortex. Archs. Gerontol. Geriatrics 1994;19:303–12.
62. Amenta F, Bronzetti E, Ricci A and others. Nucleus basalis magnocellularis lesions decrease histochemically reactive zinc stores in the rat brain: effect of choline alphoscerate treatment. Eur. J. Histochemistry 1995;39:281–8.
63. Bronzetti E, Felici L Amenta F. Effect of ipsilateral lesioning of the nucleus basalis magnocellularis and of L-a-glyceryl phosphorylcholine acetyltransferase and acetylcho linesterase in the rat fronto-parietal cortex. Neurosci. Letters 1993;164:47–50.
64. Lisman JE, Harris, KM. Quantal analysis and synaptic anatomy—integrating two views of hippocampal plasticity. Trends Neuroscience 1993;16:141–7.
65. Kempermann G, Wiskott L, Gage FH. Functional significance of adult neurogenesis. Curr. Opin. Neurobiology 2004;14:186-91.
66. Poo MM. Neurotrophins as synaptic modulators. Nat. Rev. Neuroscience 2001;2:24-32.

67. Taupin P. Adult neurogenesis in the mammalian central nervous system: functionality and potential clinical interest. Med Sci Monitor 2005;11:RA247–52.
68. Tuszynski MH, Thal L, Pay M and others. A Phase 1 clinical trial of nerve growth factor gene therapy for Alzheimer disease. Nature Medicine 2005;11:551–5.
69. Food and Nutrition Board, Institute of Medicine, National Academy of Sciences, USA. Dietary Reference Intakes for Thiamin, Riboflavin, Niacin, Vitamin B6, Folate, Vitamin B12, Pantothenic Acid, Biotin, and Choline. Washington, DC, USA: National Academy Press;1998.
70. Zeisel SH. Choline: Critical role during fetal development and dietary requirements in adults. Annu. Rev. Nutrition 2006;26:229–50.
71. Raloff J. Brain food: choline enters the nutritional limelight. Science News 2001 (Nov. 3);282–4.
72. Zeisel SH, Mar MH, Howe JC and others. Concentrations of choline-containing com pounds and betaine in common foods. J. Nutrition 2003;133:1302–7; U.S. Department of Agriculture (www.nal.usda.gov/fnic/foodcomp/Data/Choline).
73. de Moliner P, Abbiati G, Colombo M and others. Pharmacokinetics of choline alphoscer ate in the healthy volunteer. Le Basi Raz. Terapia 1993;23:75–80.
74. Abbiati G, Fossati T, Castiglioni C and others. Tissue and cerebral distribution and hepatic use of choline alphoscerate after oral and parenteral administration. Le Basi Raz. Terapia 1993;23:64–74.
75. Sigala S, Imperato A, Rizzonelli P and others. L-a-glycerylphosphorylcholine antago- nizes scopolamine-induced amnesia and enhances hippocampal cholinergic transmission in the rat. Eur. J. Pharmacology 1992;211:351–8.
76. Elenkov I, Wilder RL, Chrousos GP and others. The sympathetic nerve. Pharmacol. Reviews 2000;52:595–638.
77. Alberts B and others. Molecular Biology of the Cell (Fourth Edition). New York: Garland Science;2002.
78. Wissler I, Kirkpatrick CJ, Racke K. Non-neuronal acetylcholine, a locally acting molecule, widely distributed in biological systems. Pharmacol. Therapeutics 1998;77:59–79.
79. Wirthensohn G, Beck FX, Guder WG and others. Role and regulation of glycerophos phorylcholine in rat renal papilla. Pflugers Archives 1987;409:411–5.
80. Kwon ED, Zablocki K, Jung K and others. Osmoregulation of GPC: choline phospho diesterase in MDCK cells: different effects of urea and NaCl. Am. J. Physiology 1995;269:C35–C41.
81. Infante JP, Huszagh VA. Synthesis of highly unsaturated phosphatidylcholines in the development of sperm motility: a role for epididymal glycerol-3-phosphorylcholine. Mol. Cell. Biochemistry 1985;69:3–6.
82. Tserng KY, Griffin RL. Phosphatidylcholine de novo synthesis and modification are carried out sequentially in HL60 cells: evidence from mass isotopomer distribution analysis. Biochemistry 2004;43:8125–35.
83. Infante JP, Kirwan RC, Brenna JT. High levels of docosahexaenoic acid (22:6n-3)– containing phospholipids in high-frequency contraction muscles of hummingbirds and rattlesnakes. Comp. Biochem. Physiology (B) 2001;130:291–8.
84. Infante JP, Huszagh VA. Mechanisms of resistance to pathogenesis in muscular dystrophies. Molec. Cell. Biochemistry 1999;195:155–67.
85. Sharma U, Atri S, Sharma MC and others. Skeletal muscle metabolism in Duchenne Muscular Dystrophy (DMD): an in-vitro proton NMR spectroscopy study. Mag. Reson. Imaging 2003;21:145–53.
86. Burt CT, Ribolow H. Glycerol phosphorylcholine (GPC) and serine ethanolamine phosphodiester (SEP): evolutionary mirrored metabolites and their potential metabolic roles. Comp. Biochem. Physiology 1994;108B:11–20.
87. Hamamah S, Seguin F, Barthelemy C and others. 1H nuclear magnetic resonance studies of seminal plasma from fertile and infertile men. J. Reprod. Fertility 1993;97:51–5.

88. Hamamah S and others. Quantification by magnetic resonance spectroscopy of metabolites in seminal plasma able to differentiate different forms of azoospermia. Hum. Reproduction 1998;13:132–5.
89. Nicholson R, Calamera JC. GPC diesterase activity in human endometrial secretion. Intl. J. Fertility 1976;21:176–82.
90. Rohde P. Personal communication. Carlsbad, CA, USA:Science and Ingredients, Inc., tel 760-268-0613, www.phospholipidsonline.com; 2007.
91. Ferini Stramba L, Zucconi M, Castronovo V and others. Choline alfoscerate: short-term effect on sleep in healthy subjects. Curr. Ther. Research 1991;49:610–5.
92. Fallbrook A, Turenne SD, Mamalias N and others. Phosphatidylcholine and phosphatidylethanolamine metabolites may regulate brain phospholipid catabolism via inhibition of lysophospholipase activity. Brain Research 1999;834:207–10.
93. Krasnoperova MG. Use of cholinomimetics in the treatment of endogenous autism in children [translated from the Russian]. Zhurnal nevrologii i psikhiatrii 2004;6:35–9.

Appendix

Trials with Injected
GPC
(GlyceroPhosphoCholine)

Parris M. Kidd, PhD
www.dockidd.com
dockidd@dockidd.com

Indications for GPC as Injectable

- Stroke recovery
- Post-surgical encephalopathy
- Memory loss and other cognitive difficulties
- Personality deterioration, social withdrawal
- Growth hormone/anterior pituitary revitalization
- Craniocerebral injury (hematomas, contusions, concussions)

Product Form
GPC Injectable is supplied in a 20 cc multidose vial that delivers 500 mg ultrapure GPC per cc. The typical injection dose is 1000 mg given once daily, preferably in the morning, and is extremely well tolerated. GPC Injectable is available exclusively from College Pharmacy in Colorado Springs, Colorado.

A total of 15 published clinical trials and other human studies with injected GPC are reviewed herein. Whatever the route of administration, GPC acts rapidly and with no major adverse effects.

Pharmacokinetics in Healthy Subjects

De Moliner et al, 1993[1]
This was a pharmacokinetic study of i.m., i.v., and oral dosing with GPC. Four healthy volunteer subjects aged 19–24 years received GPC 1000 mg by i.v., then subsequently by i.m., then by mouth, then received a placebo by mouth, in four separate sessions separated by one-week washouts. During each session blood was sampled periodically over 10 hours.

With i.v. administration of GPC, plasma total choline peaked at 5 minutes and returned to baseline by 4 hours. With i.m. administration, plasma total choline peaked at 0.5 hours and returned to baseline by 6 hours. With oral GPC, plasma total choline peaked at 3 hours, at a concentration slightly less than half that reached by i.m. administration. But with oral GPC the plasma total choline remained above baseline at 10 hours. The investigators concluded that i.v. and i.m. GPC both delivered virtually identical total plasma doses (AUC, Area Under the Curve), and that oral administration delivered about half this amount.

Stroke Trials

Stroke initiates localized and spreading cell destruction that involves cell membrane breakdown, phospholipid catabolism, and metabolic dysregulation. GPC is known to protect against all these adverse processes. Five trials were conducted with GPC, altogether involving almost 3,000 stroke victims. All the patients were started on GPC 10 days after their stroke. The usual regimen was 1 month of intramuscular GPC (1,000 mg, once per day) followed by 5 months of oral intake (1,200 mg, taken between meals). GPC markedly improved the pace and extent of recovery. All aspects of memory, cognition, mood, word fluency, sociability, and overall clinical status were subject to improvement by this 6-month GPC regimen.

Consoli et al, 1993[2]

This study involved 172 patients aged 45–85 years, recruited from 20 centers distributed throughout Italy. All the patients had suffered cerebral ischemic attacks (stroke or TIA) within the previous 10 days. This could not be a placebo-controlled trial because the patients were too severely afflicted. After clinical examination was completed, the patients were evaluated by the Modified Mathew Scale for focal neurological deficits. Those with dementia, chronic neurological pathologies, or disabling psychiatric disorders, were excluded.

The Mathew Scale was developed by Mathew and collaborators in 1972 (Lancet ii, 1327–29) to more objectively assess the functional state of patients after stroke. The scoring is based on neurological examination (speech, cranial nerves, motor power, reflexes and sensation); and mental examination (levels of consciousness and orientation, performance), and scored from 0 (worst) to 100 (best).

In this trial, treatment proceeded in two phases. First, starting by day 10 following the event, GPC was given by injection to stem the deficits. After a month, GPC treatment was switched to oral supplementation for better patient compliance. In the first phase, the patients received GPC 1000 mg i.m. daily for 28 days. The second treatment phase was GPC 1200 mg by mouth (400 mg 3 times per day; 2 capsules at 8 am then 1 cap at 4 p.m.), for 5 more months. By completion of the first phase (week 4 of GPC i.m.), on the Modified Mathew Scale the percentage of patients who scored normal or had only mildly impaired performance-disability moved from 34%

to 68%, with improvements in level of consciousness, space-time orientation, speech, facial paralysis, and motor capacity.

During the second phase of this trial (GPC oral, for 5 months), three assessment scales were used. On the MMSE (Mini Mental State Examination), which judges cognitive functions, there was significant improvement (p<0.01). On the SCAG Scale (Sandoz Clinical Assessment Geriatric), there were significant improvements in cognitive dysfunction, interpersonal relations, affective disturbances (mood), apathy and isolation, and somatic disturbances (p<0.01 in all cases). On the GDS (Global Deterioration Scale), only about 100 patients were assessed but there was a clear pattern of improvement. GPC was judged excellent or good by 79% of the patients, while 71% of the patients were judged similarly improved by their physicians. Tolerability was judged excellent or good by 98% of the patients, and at 99% by the clinicians. One patient dropped out due to persistent insomnia.

Aguglia et al, 1993[3]

This also was an Italian multicenter trial, and involved 425 patients aged 45–85 years, recruited from 44 centers distributed throughout the country. All the patients had suffered cerebral ischemic attacks (stroke, TIA or acute cerebral ischemia) within the previous 10 days. It was another open trial, since the patients were too severely afflicted to be subjected to placebo treatment. Patients who scored 35 or below on the Mathew Scale were eligible for the trial, but not comatose patients or others not expected to live or judged unable to comply over the 6-month tenure of the trial.

As per the typical GPC stroke protocol, treatment proceeded in two phases, first giving GPC 1000 mg i.m. in-hospital daily for 28 days then switching to GPC 1200 mg by mouth for 5 more months (400 mg 3 times per day). Upon completion of the GPC i.m. phase, on the Mathew Scale there was an average improvement of 18.56% (11.5 points, from 62.02 to 73.53). This was statistically highly significant over baseline. A 20% or greater improvement was seen in 168 (39.5%) of the patients. By this measure the more impaired, older patients (65–85 years) were more likely to benefit than were the younger patients (45–64 years).

During the second phase, after discharge (GPC oral, for 5 months), evaluation was based on clinical interviews and three assessment scales were used. On the MMSE for cognitive functions, there was a 12.3% improvement (from 21.53 at week 5 to 24.19 at

6 months). A 20% or greater improvement was seen in 126 patients (29.7%). On the Global Deterioration Scale, there was an average 20.2% improvement. A 20% or greater improvement was seen in 180 patients (42.3%). On the Crichton Geriatric Rating Scale, which assesses mainly behavioral functioning, there was an average 19.5% improvement. A 20% or greater improvement was seen in 166 patients (39.1%).

The researchers judged GPC to be effective and well tolerated both parenterally and orally. They noted that despite the many drugs with which GPC was co-administered, no single GPC-drug interaction was observed clinically or in laboratory tests. GPC's benefits were consistent, and spanned functional state as well as performance and social behavior. With the possible exception of the MMSE (at 12.3%), the degrees of improvement from GPC on the various scales were well above that expected from a placebo, namely 12% in at least 20% of such patients.

Barbagallo Sangiorgi et al, 1994[4]

This study involved 2,044 patients aged 45–85 years, recruited from 176 centers in Italy. All had suffered cerebral ischemic attacks (stroke or TIA) within the previous 10 days. Most patients (87.1%) had concurrent diseases, mostly cardiovascular. Once again, this could not be a placebo-controlled trial because the patients were too severely afflicted. A minimal 35% degree of consciousness (35 on the Mathew Scale) was necessary for inclusion in the study. Patients were further classified into "more deteriorated" (Mathew 35–65) and "less deteriorated" (Mathew >65).

The usual neurological assessments and blood chemistries were done, and the patients received conventional treatment for stroke. As per the prevailing protocol, treatment was in two phases, the first phase being GPC 1000 mg i.m. daily for 28 days then the second phase being 1200 mg by mouth for 5 more months. After the first phase a high percentage (47%) of the patients moved from being more deteriorated to less deteriorated (p<0.001). During the second phase, on the MMSE (cognitive functions) there was an average 15.7% increase as the 60% of patients with "abnormal deterioration" at day 28 fell to 35% at 6 months. Using the Crichton Geriatric Rating Scale (behavioral), there was an average 25.8% improvement. The count of patients with severe deterioration fell from 9.8% at day 28 to 2 percent at 6 months; those with moderate deterioration, from 30.4% to 14.3%; and those with mild deterioration jumped from 59.8% to 83.7 percent. On the Global Deterioration Scale there was an average 25.9% improvement during the second phase.

At the end of the first phase of this trial (28 days) the investigators judged that 94% of the patients showed very good to moderate improvement. At 6 months, the end of the second phase, this fraction was still 95%, with clinically significant improvements in cognition, behavior, and overall condition. Of an original 2,056 treated patients, 14 (0.68%) withdrew due to adverse effects, their problems being mostly heartburn, nausea, or overexcitation.

Gambi and Onofrj, 1994[5]

This was another open trial, conducted similarly to the foregoing trials. A total of 320 patients aged 40–85 years were recruited from 34 centers in Italy; all were suffering from mental deficits following cerebral ischemic attack. Again, there were the two phases: GPC 1000 mg i.m. once daily for 28 days, then 1200 mg by mouth for another 5 months. In the first phase, GPC significantly improved patients on the Mathew scale of consciousness by week 2 ($p<0.0001$). By the end of the second phase, at 6 months, there was highly significantly improvement of the patient population on the MMSE, on the SCAG, and on the Global Deterioration Scale (GDS).

The MMSE scores showed marked recovery of cognitive-memory functions by 6 months ($p<0.0001$). Similarly on the SCAG, the total scale and all the subscales—cognitive dysfunction, interpersonal relationships, affective disturbances, apathy/isolation, and somatic disturbances—were highly significantly improved between week 5 and 6 months ($p<0.0001$). The GDS scores on confusion and other dementia-like symptoms also markedly improved over the second phase, indicating an overall lessening of the severity of the mental decline ($p<0.0001$).

These physicians concurred that about 70% of the patients were "excellent" or "good" by the 6-month mark. GPC's tolerability was judged excellent or good in more than 90% of the patients, the main problem in the first phase being dizziness and in the second, stomach upset. They concluded that altogether, the cognitive and global clinical assessment scales showed a "large improvement" of the mental status of the patients. They praised "a considerable contraction" in the normal recovery times for stroke during the first 2 weeks of the first phase, also stating:

The marked resolution in 4 weeks of focal neurological deficits, particularly regarding space-time orientation, degree of consciousness, language, motor capacity and degree of invalidity...leads us to think that GPC is an optimum therapeutic choice...The changes recorded over the 5 months (of the second phase) represents an attainment of an acceptable quality of life for the patients. [Discussion][5]

Tomasina et al, 1991[6]
This was a small open trial that followed the usual GPC stroke protocol. Eleven patients of average age 74 years received GPC 1000 mg i.m. once daily for 28 days, then 1200 mg by mouth daily for at least another 20 weeks. On various rating scales (Mathew, MMSE, SCAG, the Psychic Evaluation Scale) GPC significantly improved memory, anxiety, emotional lability, sociability, spatial orientation, and aspects of language; eye deviation; confusion, vigilance, and general mental sharpness. Two patients complained of a slight, transitory heartburn but did not withdraw from the trial. At 6 months the physicians judged 10/11 of the patients as excellent to fairly good, while 10/10 patients judged themselves as excellent to fairly good.

Thus, in 5 open trials completed by 2,972 patients variously afflicted by stroke, a regimen of 1 month of intramuscular GPC followed by 5 months of oral intake produced clinically remarkable improvement. Given that the patients were generally too ill to be given placebos, the degrees of clinical improvement over the 6-month trial durations were well above those predictable as placebo effects. Many patients showed accelerated improvement within the first 2–4 weeks then continued to improve over the remaining 5 months. The physicians as well as the patients uniformly judged GPC to be very well tolerated.

Cognitive Decline Trials
Cognitive decline resulting from vascular or Alzheimer's dementia, to "senile organic brain syndrome," or from injury, involves neural circuit breakdown linked to oxidative and/or inflammatory processes and perhaps also to excitotoxic damage. Similar to stroke, the cell-level degeneration features cell membrane breakdown, phospholipid catabolism, and metabolic dysregulation. In 5 trials that involved a total of 388 patients, GPC given i.m. improved memory and other cognitive functions, interpersonal relationships, and word

fluency. The regimen was 1 gram of intramuscular GPC (1,000 mg), once per day, for 3 months.

Vascular dementia patients were recruited into a series of 3 randomized, controlled trials, very similarly designed but carried out by 3 different groups in Italy. GPC i.m. was compared against citicoline (CDP-choline) i.m. GPC proved superior in all three trials.

Muratorio et al, 1992[7]
Multi-infarct (vascular) dementia, mild to moderate. Ninety-seven (97) patients were randomized to receive GPC 1000 mg i.m. or citicoline 1000 mg i.m., once daily for 90 days/3 months. Seventy-three (73) patients completed the 90-day follow-up period. CDP-choline significantly improved only word fluency, which benefit persisted into follow up. GPC significantly improved ALL the measures of dementia, including memory (by 30 days) and other cognition measures, behavior, and disability. GPC's benefits all persisted into follow up.

Frattola et al, 1991[8]
Multi-infarct (vascular) dementia, mild to moderate. A total 117 patients were randomized to receive GPC 1000 mg i.m. or citicoline 1000 mg i.m., once daily for 90 days/3 months. Both agents significantly improved memory, other cognition, and behavior, but GPC had earlier onset and was significantly more beneficial for memory, other cognitive functions, interpersonal relationships, and word fluency.

DiPerri et al, 1991[9]
Multi-infarct (vascular) dementia, mild to moderate. A total 115 patients were randomized to receive GPC 1000 mg i.m. or citicoline 1000 mg i.m. once daily in the morning for 90 days/3 months. Both nutrients significantly improved memory, mood, and behavior, but GPC proved significantly more beneficial over citicoline.

Schettini et al, 1993[10]
Probable Alzheimer's patients, double-blind trial. Nineteen (19) patients older than 60 years received GPC 1000 mg i.m. or a placebo once daily for 3 months (12 weeks). In addition to neuropsychological assessment, blood hormone levels—cortisol, ACTH, prolactin, growth hormone (GH)—were measured, at baseline and at 3 months.

The SCAG total score was significantly improved by GPC over the placebo, at 3 months; the subscales for cognitive disturbances and apathy/isolation also showed significant improvement. Interestingly, GPC significantly reduced plasma cortisol and ACTH levels over the placebo, but not prolactin. Growth hormone levels were significantly increased over baseline at 12 weeks; the placebo group had fallen below baseline.

Brain SPECT scanning (single-photon emission computed tomography) was conducted on 9 of the GPC and 9 of the placebo patients, also at baseline and at the 3-month mark. None of those on placebo showed an increase; rather, on average there was a decrease. Of the GPC patients 4/9 showed a >7% increase in cerebral blood flow, over the entire cerebrum including the temporal-parietal zones.

The investigators that GPC could be useful for down-regulating HPAA (hypothalamic pituitary adrenal axis) over-activation, which can contribute to neurodegenerative progression. The increase in GH was clinically meaningful.

Abbati et al, 1991[11]
Forty (40) patients with "senile organic brain syndrome" were randomized to receive GPC 1000 mg i.m. or oxiracetam 1000 mg i.m., once daily at 8 am for 12 weeks/3 months. Both agents improved cognition, behavior, and reaction time. GPC showed significant improvement after 6 weeks, with further improvement at weeks 8 and 12. GPC lagged behind oxiracetam for the first 8 weeks, then caught up with oxiracetam and maintained its benefits significantly longer, 8 weeks after treatment was discontinued.

The encouraging outcomes of these trials with intramuscular GPC are reminiscent of others conducted on cognitive decline patients with GPC given by mouth. However, increase of serum growth hormone levels after giving only GPC by mouth has not yet been unequivocally demonstrated.

Growth Hormone Potentiation
It is well established that blood growth hormone levels undergo dramatic decline as humans enter middle age, and that such decline is linked to aging. Attempts to revitalize fading functions by injecting GH itself tend to generate undesirable effects. An ortho-molecular—metabolic intervention that successfully elevates GH via endogenous release would have great value for healthy aging. Intravenous GPC is such an intervention.

Several papers were published on this subject by one research group. Three protocols were followed, each utilizing intravenous GPC to potentiate GHRH stimulation of GH release.

Ceda et al, 1994[12]

This paper was the last published, and conveniently includes all 3 protocols. The subjects for each protocol were drawn from a pool of healthy young (n=8) and elderly (n=17) volunteers. Blood GH was measured following an i.v. injection of 1 microgram per kilogram of GHRH (Growth Hormone Releasing Hormone) that was preceded by injection of GPC or placebo.

In one protocol, GPC at either 2000 mg or 1000 mg was injected i.v., followed immediately by GHRH injection, into young and old subjects. GPC significantly enhanced GH release into the blood, with the 1000 mg dose seemingly as effective as the 2000 mg dose.

In a second protocol, GHRH was injected i.v. twice into elderly subjects, with a 120 minute interval between the 2 GHRH injections. Fifteen (15) minutes before the second GHRH bolus was given, GPC 2000 mg was injected i.v. This GPC shot significantly potentiated GH responsiveness to the second GHRH stimulation, as compared against GHRH given twice by itself.

The third protocol was a subacute one, and used elderly subjects. Every day for 15 days, first GPC 2000 mg was injected i.v., then came the standard GHRH injection. Normally these repeated daily injections of GHRH would blunt the GH secretory response. In this experiment, GPC blocked the blunting effect of repeated GHRH.

These protocols establish the efficacy of intravenous GPC to potentiate GH release. They also gibe with the above-described double-blind study by Schettini et al, in which 3 months of daily i.m. GPC injections raised blood GH levels. Altogether, these findings indicate GPC acutely potentiates GHRH, the physiologic GH releaser from the hypothalamus; and that GPC might prove useful to facilitate endogenous GH availability on an ongoing daily basis.

Brain Injury Trials

In this category three studies were located. One involved heart surgery survivors. Two reported on patients with subdural hematomas, cerebral contusions, or concussions. Of these latter, one successfully employed GPC i.v. in very high doses for comatose patients.

Auteri et al, 1993[13]

Some 50-60% of cardiac bypass and other open heart surgery survivors emerge from the anesthesia with amnesic or other cognitive difficulties. Some recover within days or weeks, others suffer permanent disablement. In addition to memory difficulties, mental fatigue is common and also changes in affect and personality, rather resembling a diffuse post-surgical encephalopathy. This small trial was conducted double-blind, and successfully utilized GPC both i.v. AND i.m.

Post-cardiac bypass patients were studied. Twenty (20) patients aged 45-65 years were randomized into two groups. Cognitive functions were tested using the Wechsler Memory Scale, the Benton Visual Retention Test, and the Wechsler Adult Intelligence Scale. One group received GPC, 1000 mg i.v. once daily for 4 weeks, then 1000 mg i.m. once daily for another 5 months, to total 6 months of treatment. The other group received a placebo.

Significant changes were found on the Wechsler Memory Scale. Already by the 4 week timepoint, GPC had benefited memory significantly over the placebo. By the 24 week/6 month final timepoint, there was a striking superiority of GPC compared to the placebo. While the patients on placebo continued to exhibit decline throughout the trial, at 6 months the GPC patients had reversed their decline and returned almost to baseline.

Mandat et al, 2003[14]

The trauma of craniocerebral injury (CCI) produces metabolic disturbances that are likely to include mixed ischemic-hypoxic, oxidative, inflammatory, and excitotoxic cascades. This study evaluated the risk and efficacy of GPC ("choline alfoscerate," CA) in 23 CCI patients. Of these, 8 had acute hematoma with multiple hemorrhagic foci, of which 7 were operated on with extreme urgency and one later. Another 6 had cerebral contusion with multiple hemorrhagic foci, and 9 patients had concussions. At admission, 11 patients were assessed at 8 points on the ATS (Adult Trauma Scale); 4 scored at 9 on the ATS; and 8 scored at 11 on the ATS.

The approach was 2-phase, similar to the protocol for stroke management. Patients were evaluated on the ATS or the Karnofsky Scale at admission, then at days 1, 2, 5, and 14 following the injury, and at 2 and 3 months following the injury. GPC was administered at 1000 mg per day i.m. for 14 days, then at 800 mg per day by mouth for 28 days.

After 3 months, 96% of the patients had improved. Fourteen patients (61%, including ATS admission scores of 9 and 11) were independent and professionally active, at 90–100% on the Karnofsky Scale. Five (22%) were independent but did not work (70-80% Karnofsky); three (13%) required permanent care (40–60% Karnofsky). No complications from GPC were observed.

This paper is notable both for the degree of difficulty of the cases treated, and for the low oral GPC intake that was used: 800 mg per day, one-third lower than the oral doses used in the other trials. That 96% (22 of 23) of these seriously injured patients could respond over the 3-month period to only 2 weeks of i.m. GPC and such a low oral intake, suggests the simple GPC molecule may be very strong medicine.

Madorskyi S, Amcheslavskyi V, 1994 (abstract report only)[15]
These clinicians, working at the famed Burdenko Neurosurgical Institute in Moscow, studied the effects of GPC on the dynamics of consciousness recovery and brain bioelectrical activity in comatose patients with head injury (HI). Investigation was carried out in 25 comatose patients on day 3–14 after HI. GPC was given intravenously at 150 mg/kg (equivalent to 10.5 grams of GPC per 154-lb patient), and the results compared against a control group. Judging from the Glasgow Coma Scale, GPC effected earlier emergence from the Coma State (on the 3rd day on average), less speech impairment, and more effective regress of focal neurological symptoms than for controls. Using EEG spectral power mapping and coherence analyses, the researchers concluded GPC tended to normalize cerebral blood flow, decrease vascular resistance, and improve spontaneous brain bioelectrical activity along with restoration of circuits. This trial, unfortunately available only in abstract form, seems to suggest that very high doses of GPC are safe for injection, and that GPC can be effective even for patients who are comatose following head injury.

Closing Comments
In all the 15 trials reviewed above, injected GPC proved effective and safe to take, with minor adverse effects that rarely forced withdrawal from the studies, even with fragile patient populations. The most common regimen was daily intramuscular injection of 1,000 mg GPC, usually in the morning, for 30 days; then oral supplementation with 1200 mg GPC daily for another 5 months. GPC as a dietary supplement is best taken in a single dose before breakfast, and/or between breakfast and lunch in 2 divided doses.

GPC is compatible with drugs in common use by the elderly,[13] but being a cholinergic agent may not be fully compatible with high doses of cholinergic drugs. As an injectable, GPC has remarkable potential for stroke management and for accelerating recovery from virtually any brain injury as well as for the other indications listed in a foregoing section.

Injectable GPC as provided is highly stable and easily buffered in the syringe. The multidose vials provided by College Pharmacy supply GPC 500 mg/cc, total 20 cc. For i.m. administration, simply draw 2 cc (1000 mg GPC) and administer as is. For i.v use, mix 2 cc (1000 mg GPC) into 50–100 ml normal saline, lactated Ringer, or dextrose 5% in water, then run it in over 15–30 minutes.

GPC has been safely used by i.m. injection in the many clinical studies just described. GPC was administered by i.v. injection into the postsurgical, elderly heart patients at 1000 mg per day for 4 weeks; into young and old healthy subjects for the growth hormone studies, at up to 2000 mg per day for 15 days; and supposedly into comatose, brain-injured patients at 150 mg per kilogram body weight for at least 3 days.

Although GPC is relatively stable to oxidation, no information is available on giving GPC by injection along with oxidants like ozone and peroxide. Also, since GPC raises blood choline it is relatively contraindicated with anticholinergic drugs. Still, for patients being maintained on such protocols additional benefits from GPC could be anticipated. Here I suggest titrating the GPC orally (high-quality 300 mg hardgel capsules are available from College Pharmacy), increasing the dose from 300 mg per day to 600 mg per day then 1200 mg per day over 3–4 weeks.

GPC's very high degree of safety is undoubtedly related to its being an orthomolecule, and additionally a major physiological antitoxin for the kidney, liver, brain and probably all the organs.

GPC's diverse applications for cognitive decline and stroke were earlier reviewed in 2001 by the veteran researcher Lucilla Parnetti.[16] This review covers additional trials that were not yet available at that time. GPC's diverse applications as a dietary supplement are further documented in my more extensive review article that accompanies this one.[17,18] This latter review more specifically explores GPC's clinical applications as a dietary supplement, the putative mechanisms by which the GPC orthomolecule can have such remarkable efficacy and safety, and other aspects of GPC's uniqueness for active living and healthy aging.[18]

References Numbered in the Appendix

1. de Moliner P, et al. Pharmacokinetics of choline alphoscerate in the healthy volunteer. *Le Basi Raz Ter* 1993;23 (Suppl. 3):75.
2. Consoli D, et al. The use of alpha-GPC in patients with acute cerebrovascular accident. *Archivio di Medicina Interna* 1993; 45:13.
3. Aguglia E, et al. Choline alphoscerate in the treatment of mental pathology following acute cerebrovascular accident. *Functional Neurol* Supplement 3, 1993;8:5.
4. Barbagallo Sangiorgi G, et al. alpha-glycerophosphocholine in the mental recovery of cerebral ischemic attacks. *Ann N Y Acad Sci* 1994;717:253.
5. Gambi D, Onofrj M. Multicenter clinical study of efficacy and tolerability of choline alfoscerate in patients with deficits in higher mental function arising after an acute ischemic cerebrovascular attack.*Geriatria* 1994;6:91.
6. Tomasina C, et al. Clinical study of the therapeutic effectiveness and tolerability of choline alfoscerate in 15 subjects with compromised cognitive functions subsequent to acute focal cerebral ischemia. *Rivista Neuropsi Sci Affini* 1996;37:21.
7. Muratorio A, et al. A neurotropic approach to the treatment of multi-infarct dementia using L-alpha-glycerylphosphorylcholine. *Curr Ther Res* 1992;52:741.
8. Frattola L, et al. Multicenter clinical comparison of the effects of choline alfoscerate and cytidine diphosphocholine in the treatment of multi-infarct dementia. *Curr Therap Res* 1991;49:683.
9. Di Perri R, et al. A multicentre trial to evaluate the efficacy and tolerability of alpha-glycerylphosphorylcholine versus cytosine diphospho choline in patients with vascular dementia. *J Intl Med Res* 1991;19:330.
10. Schettini G, et al. Effect of choline alfoscerate in elderly patients with primary degenerative dementia. *Le Basi Raz Ter* 1993;23 (Suppl. 3):108.
11. Abbati C, et al. Nootropic therapy of cerebral aging. *Adv Therapy* 1991;8:268.
12. Ceda GP, et al. Effects of an acetylcholine precursor on GH secretion in elderly subjects. In: Bercu, BB, Walker, RF, eds. *Growth Hormone II: Basic and Clinical Aspects.* Springer-Verlag;1994.
13. Auteri A, et al. Protecting the brain during heart surgery: treatment with choline alfoscerate. *Le Basi Raz Ter* 1993;23 (Suppl. 3):123.
14. Mandat T, et al. A preliminary evaluation of risk and efficacy of early choline alphoscerate treatment in craniocerebral injury. *Neurol Neurochir Pol* 2003;37:1231-1238.
15. Madorskyi S, Amcheslavskyi V. GPC in treatment of consciousness disorders after head injury. *Neuropsychopharmacol* 1994;10(3S):8S (abstract only).
16. Parnetti L, et al. Choline alphoscerate in cognitive decline and in acute cerebrovascular disease: an analysis of published clinical data. *Mechs Ageing Dev* 2001;122:2041.
17. Kidd PM. GlyceroPhosphoCholine (GPC), mind-body nutrient for active living and healthy aging. 2005: Carlsbad, California, USA: Science and Ingredients, Inc., tel. 760-268-0613, www.Science&Ingredients.com, www.PhospholipidsOnline.com
18. Address for technical correspondence: Parris M. Kidd, PhD, dockidd@dockidd.com

The Future of Phospholipids as Dietary Supplements

A Letter from Peter Rohde, CEO, Science & Ingredients, Inc.

During the more than twenty years since I teamed up with Dr. Kidd, educating the public about phospholipids has always been our commitment. Our work continues. Though "phospholipid" is a word quite well known to the dietary supplement industry, it still has not yet reached the level of being a "household name".

Following on our first book in this series, titled *PS (PhosphatidylSerine), Nature's Brain Booster for Memory, Mood and Stress,* this book is another step in that direction. Our next book will be on omega-3 phospholipids. These are phospholipids that have omega-3 fatty acids as part of their molecular structure.

Marine substances will play a major role in the future. There are certain fish and crustacean sources, which are particularly rich in phospholipids. One omega-3 phospholipid product that holds great promise is from krill. Krill is a hardy, shrimp-like creature abundant in all the oceans. The krill of the coldest oceans have the highest amounts of omega-3 long-chain fatty acids—EPA (eicosapentaenoic acid) and DHA (docosahexaenoic acid). The Antarctic krill survive Earth's coldest waters by having a lot of omega-3s in their cell membranes. These are structurally integrated with the membrane phospholipids and help the membranes continue to work even when it's very cold outside.

Krill has a wide range of desirable nutritional properties and is a traditional food in Japan. Krill can be processed to produce phospholipid complexes highly enriched in the omega-3 fatty acid. Built into these molecular complexes is a high content of astaxanthin. This is a rare and highly potent carotenoid nutrient, which also has anti-inflammatory properties.

Whether in krill cell membranes or in those of humans, the three most important types of cell membrane nutrients—phospholipids, omega-3 fatty acids, antioxidants—are keys to homeostasis, the processes that maintain the conditions necessary for life. They sustain the cell membrane systems that manage the internal cell environment. For any living being, maintaining cell membrane integrity is the "bottom-line" prerequisite for survival.

Properly manufactured, krill phospholipids are very good stuff. In clinical trials krill oil was directly compared against fish oil and found to be far more potent than the EPA and DHA in fish oils. Fish oils have very little phospholipid and their omega-3s are almost totally in the form of triglycerides (fat storage forms, as in adipose tissue). Animal experiments established that omega-3s attached to phospholipids are far more clinically potent, dose for dose, than they are as triglycerides.

Clinical researchers continue to discover new and fascinating functions of the omega-3s EPA and DHA as dietary supplements. Both are essential for fetal and early childhood development. Both improve behavioral and mood disorders. EPA and DHA both counter pro-inflammatory processes that drive degenerative joint, circulatory, digestive, and brain diseases. The powerful antioxidants in krill also render it exceptionally stable against oxidation, and contribute to its synergistic nutritional benefits.

The carotenoid astaxanthin, small amounts of vitamin A and vitamin E, and a novel bioflavonoid in krill oil all contribute to its exceptional stability and antioxidant potency. Its high ORAC value (Oxygen Radical Absorbance Capacity) is a measure of its capacity to block free radicals that could otherwise cause great toxic harm.

Another next-generation phospholipid dietary supplement is omega-3 PS (PhosphatidylSerine). PS is an essential building block for all cell membranes but is especially abundant in brain cells. Every cell is surrounded by an outer "cell membrane" that separates its living interior from its nonliving outer environment. This membrane contains transfer proteins that help control what molecules enter the cell and what molecules are allowed to leave. These membranes need PS to help them stay efficient and conserve precious life energy.

PS is also needed for the membranes of the mitochondria, which are the cell's energy boilers. The mitochondria churn out lots of ATP which is the universal energy molecule—the "energy currency of life".

PS is an especially important building block for the nerve cell membranes that manage the packaging, release, and actions of the brain's many chemical transmitters. Those directly influenced by PS include acetylcholine, dopamine, adrenaline, noradrenaline, serotonin, and GABA. These and many other transmitters rely on little "antennas" located on the brain cells and called receptors. For these to work they must have PS in the membrane that is built around them.

Some of the PS molecules in our brain cells carry omega-3 DHA and/or EPA within their molecular structure. DHA and EPA give very high fluidity and other desirable properties to the membrane, and help optimize membrane protein functions. For nerve cells located in the brain or even outside the brain, these features are keys to optimal function.

Until very recently, PS with omega-3s attached was not available as a dietary supplement. In the very early days of research with PS, the only such "omega-3 PS" was prepared from cow brain. But as "mad cow disease" spread, this source became no longer sufficiently safe and reliable. In its place, PS was made from soy lecithin. Soy PS had very little DHA or EPA attached. Now the technology exists to produce omega-3 PS.

Several technologies can be used. One way is to pull other fatty acids off the PS molecule and substitute them with omega-3s like EPA and DHA. Now, with PS, EPA and DHA "conjugated" in one molecule there is the opportunity to create a new generation of powerful brain supplements and neuroceuticals. A different technology is to use marine phospholipids with the omega-3s and convert the given phospholipids into PS using enzymatic processes. The result is a synergistic potency of PS and omega-3's, which potentially can benefit ALL the organ systems of the body.

In a double-blind clinical trial on children with attentional and behavior problems, such a conjugated "Omega-3 PS" produced marked benefits on a variety of test measures. Its extent of benefit was far greater than from fish oil, and was comparable with the most effective pharmaceuticals available for these problems. Animal experiments suggest that when omega-3s are conjugated to phospholipids, greater amounts of them reach the brain following dosing by mouth. Fatty acids linked into phospholipids are more bioavailable and more potent than those not associated with phospholipids.

We see a clear trend for future phospholipid product development. Phospholipids, underrated and relatively unnoticed for a long time, finally are stepping out of the shadows. They will eventually win mainstream recognition, not only for cognition and the other higher functions of the brain, but also for a variety of other body functions.

PS and other phospholipids when associated with the omega-3 fatty acids DHA and EPA are truly the building blocks for life. GPC seems to be used by our cells as a preferred nucleus for making omega-3 PC (PhosphatidylCholine). We at Science and Ingredients are proud to be at the forefront of exploring the benefits of all phospholipids for mental and physical performance, for active living and for a healthy aging process.

Peter Rohde
Chief Executive Officer
Science and Ingredients, Inc.